ELECTRIFYING THE UNDERGROUND

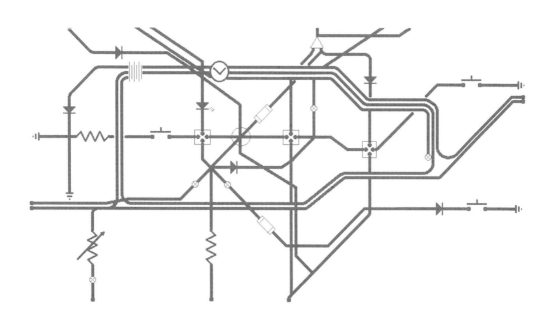

ELECTRIFYING THE UNDERGROUND

The technology that created London's Tube

Graeme Gleaves

AMBERLEY

First published 2014

Amberley Publishing
The Hill, Stroud
Gloucestershire, GL5 4EP

www.amberley-books.com

British Library Cataloguing in Publication Data.
A catalogue record for this book is available from the British Library.

ISBN 978 1 4456 2203 3
e-book ISBN 978 1 4456 2219 4

Typeset in 10pt on 12pt Sabon.
Typesetting and Origination by Amberley Publishing.
Printed in the UK.

Contents

1938 stock train arrives at Queens Park with a northbound Bakerloo service on 9 May 1985.
These units were in the twilight of their careers by this time and had become an icon of travel
around London. *(Basil Hancock)*

Introduction

The network of lines that criss-cross London and make up what we know today as the 'Tube' have their origins before the dawn of electricity and electric railways. The 'emission free' Underground was not what its founding fathers had in mind when they commenced construction of the system in the second half of the nineteenth century. Indeed the very first lines to be constructed came before the concept that would give it its nickname of the Tube, was developed. What brought us to where we are now is a series of advancements in technology that those who were in a position to, were wise enough to seize upon to create the world's largest, all electric, metropolitan railway network.

The London Underground is one part of daily life that is never fully appreciated until it is not there. It is estimated to have four million users every day and most of them simply assume it will remain a part of their daily routine, a means of getting from one point to another, never sparing a thought for the vast planning and organisation that is required to maintain its daily operation, let alone the feats of engineering and design that made it possible in the first place. Not only does it supply millions of workers with their transport to work, football fans with their ride to the match and back again

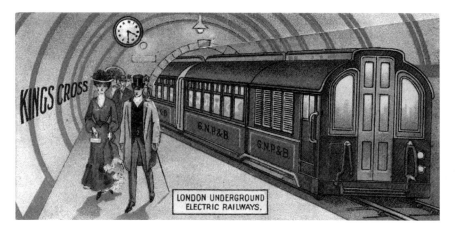

Contemporary postcard issued by the GNB&PR to promote the new service.

afterwards, tourists with the means of seeing the sights and partygoers with their designated driver; it was also an essential part of London's successful bid to host the 2012 Olympics. It would impossible to imagine getting around London without the Tube and it is as much a part of the fabric of the city as the historic landmarks it passes beneath. The Underground is also a vital part of London's economy as it provides jobs for thousands who wear the uniform, maintain the tracks or trains, and those who run the countless retail outlets at the stations.

My own interest in the Underground developed from when I was a small boy taking rare trips to London, trying to find my way around the map that at first looked impossible to navigate. Since then I have become a regular traveller over some sections, I have ended up driving the trains over others and I have been a sometime resident of various parts of London on the Ungerground network. The Underground has been a part of my life for as long as I can remember and will far outlive me.

In this book I have attempted to tell the story of how the Underground developed. The journey from an ambitious concept in the nineteenth century to the present system that far exceeds anything those original pioneers could have envisaged. I have aimed at a general level of interest and have avoided getting too deeply into the technical data as there are plenty of other volumes and websites that can furnish such information for those who want to know more. (Accordingly, there is a list of recommended further reading at the end of the book.) *Electrifying the Underground* tells the story of the building of the tunnels, the electrification of the rails and the introduction and operation of some of the most innovative electric trains of their age.

Graeme Gleaves

Chapter 1

Steam in the Sewers

London in the mid-nineteenth century was arguably one of the most important cities on Earth, if not the most important. It was the hub of a vast empire than spanned the globe, generating trade and commerce and with it the movement of a huge number of people. It has been estimated that some three quarters of a million people of all classes made their way into and across London each working day. Some arrived on the new mainline railways that had reached into the edges of London from the mid-1830s onwards, others travelled by road in horse-drawn carriages on the cobbled roads; but the vast majority walked. Even those fortunate enough to be able to afford the luxury of public transport found that the trains could take them only so far. The main line companies were not permitted to build lines beyond a boundary imposed upon them by Parliament which stretched along the Pentonville Road and New Road (later renamed as the Euston Road) in the north and The Strand on the north bank of the Thames in the south. Between these two lines, which included the important City area, there was only the roads, and these were becoming increasingly congested not only by carriages and the new horse buses, but also the other forms of horse-drawn wagons and drays needed to convey the vast amounts of goods and materials that London needed on a daily basis. It was against this backdrop that a new and radical transportation scheme was drawn up.

The man credited with first putting forward the idea of an underground railway was one Charles Pearson, a City of London solicitor who expended vast energy in convincing those who would listen that his was the only idea that could tackle the ever growing problem of traffic congestion. It was a brave concept and Pearson met with considerable resistance. The railways were still in their infancy at the time and the vast majority of Londoners had never travelled on a train. They did not appreciate how effective the railways could be at moving large numbers of people and also goods. The only experience that the Victorians had of building underground was with the newly constructed sewers; so the notion that actually travelling beneath the surface of London was the way of the future would take a lot of hard selling. History does not record how much influence Charles Pearson had directly on those that eventually recognised the merit of building an underground railway, but by 1853 there was a credible scheme which went before Parliament to seek authority for its construction. As a result, the North Metropolitan Railway Company obtained powers to build a sub-surface railway between the Edgware Road and King's Cross. This company had absorbed the one set up by Pearson, although the man credited with first promoting the idea of an underground railway was no longer involved in seeing his dream realised. Not lacking in ambition, the North Metropolitan returned to Parliament to obtain further powers to extend the length of their proposed line.

It was in 1860 that work began. The method of construction was to become known as 'cut and cover'. This entailed excavating a huge trench which was lined with brickwork. The trench was then roofed over to form the tunnel. To minimise disruption much of the route followed existing roads and the roof of the tunnel became the new road surface, indeed many motorists in London are blissfully unaware that they are in fact driving along the roof of part of the Underground. Following the route of existing roads also avoided the burden of buying up property that the line might otherwise have passed beneath, which had been a requirement of the powers granted by parliament. Even then the cost of purchasing property in London was high! The construction work proceeded at a brisk pace despite some notable setbacks, not least the collapse of part of the works in 1862 when the Fleet Ditch Sewer was breached and flooded the works.

The new line, by then known simply as the Metropolitan Railway, opened to passengers on 10 January 1863. On this day Londoners travelled on an Underground railway for the first time on the line stretching from Farringdon Street in the east to Bishops Road (Paddington station) at the western end. Operated by the Great Western Railway who provided locomotives, carriages and the crews, the line had been built to a mixed gauge to accommodate both the GWR's 7 foot broad gauge and the narrower or standard gauge of just over 4 feet 8 inches that the other companies. It was expected that the line would connect with any other railways who would want to run services over it. Propulsion was purely by steam locomotives. It was foreseen that steam locomotives operating in confined tunnels would create a problem with a sulphurous atmosphere and measures were taken to alleviate this by building many open-air sections where the smoke and steam could escape and the fresh air could enter. In truth this became a serious problem, one that was never truly overcome while steam traction persisted, but for the early years it did not seem to matter as Londoners, or at least those who could afford it, embraced the new underground railway.

Atmospheric pollution was not the main problem faced by the Metropolitan Railway at first. Within six months of opening it had fallen out with the Great Western Railway over the planned extension of the line westward to Moorgate, with the result that the GWR pulled out of running the service along the entire line. The Metropolitan was forced to seek the assistance of the Great Northern Railway who provided an assortment of carriages and locomotives to allow the service to continue while they went about sourcing its own permanent fleet. None of this detracted from the line's early success, including the opening of the extension to Moorgate in 1865. The success of the Metropolitan had two repercussions; firstly plans were drawn up for to extend the line on three fronts and secondly it spawned an imitator on the southern side of the City.

The first of the Metropolitan extensions saw it restore its relationship with the GWR as both companies had running rights over a new line running from Hammersmith

A photograph of the surface works involved in the constructing of a cut-and-cover sub-surface line, taken at Paddington.

A GWR broad gauge train illustrated on a Metropolitan service in the area of Praed Street Junction. *(JC)*

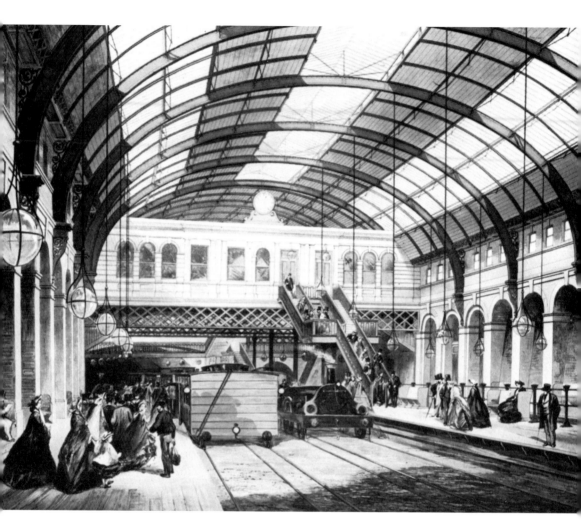

An illustration of the first operations on the Metropolitan Railway.

An original condition 4-4-0 locomotive, number 51, built by Beyer Peacock.

Broadway to link up with both the Metropolitan and the GWR at the Bishop's Road station at Paddington. Although this line had been constructed by the Hammersmith & City Railway Company, the intention from the outset was for the daily operations to be handled by the two more experienced companies. The Metropolitan's next extension would lead them to having ambitions of becoming a more mainline orientated company. In 1868 a single track line was opened from Baker Street to run through tunnels via St Johns Wood and Marlborough Road to reach Swiss Cottage. The line was operated as little more than a shuttle to start with, as no through trains ran beyond Baker Street, but this was the humble beginnings of what became the Metroland line.

The Metropolitan Railway's final extension was to the east of its original line and was opened as far as Aldgate on 18 November 1876. The construction of this section had been delayed as the result of problems with raising the sufficient finance as by this time the Metropolitan's early financial success had evaporated and it had difficulties in obtaining credit for the new work.

All of work on constructing these Metropolitan extensions work took place while a newcomer to the underground railway market, the Metropolitan and District Railway (M&DR), was establishing itself. Like the Metropolitan it saw the commercial advantage of going after the east to west traffic by following a route connecting the termini of the mainline companies. The first section of the M&DR was opened in late 1868 between Wesminster and South Kensington. For most of its route it was built by the cut and cover method along the north bank of the Thames, and by combining

M&DR locomotive showing the open cab and the air reservoirs under for the brakes.

with the construction works for the new Victoria Embankment it was extended to reach Blackfriars in 1870. By this time the Metropolitan had built a branch from Paddington through West London to South Kensington where it joined the newly built M&DR, and the first services ran on Christmas Eve 1868. The Metropolitan operated all services over both its own line and that of the M&DR using Metropolitan Railway locomotives and carriages. The M&DR made a further costly extension from Blackfriars to Mansion House which opened on 3 July 1871. The gap between the two companies was growing ever smaller and despite the obvious need for a line of just over a mile in length to link the Metropolitan at Aldgate with the M&DR at Mansion House the two companies could neither raise the finance or agree on the method of construction, so strained had relations between them become. It fell to a third party, a company formed by City financiers under the name of the Metropolitan Inner Circle Completion Company, to finally kick-start the two rivals into completing the work, which also included street improvements. Even this did not settle the disputes between the Metropolitan and M&DR who seemed to go out of their way to make life difficult for each other. Eventually common sense prevailed and London was 'encircled' for the first time by an underground railway on 6 October 1884.

During the intervening years while the disputes raged over the construction of the inner circle, the M&DR had been busy in the west of London, aiming for the new suburbs that were springing up there. They too had projected west to Hammersmith, using a route through Earls Court and West Kensington which opened in 1874. From there it took only a small link line to enable them to connect with the London &

South Western Railways (L&SWR) route to Richmond over which the M&DR gained running rights in 1877. Two further branches were constructed. The first left the main route just west of Earls Court and turned south west to West Brompton, opening in 1869. This was extended in 1880 to reach Putney Bridge and from there a new bridge was built over the River Thames to take the M&DR onward to link up with the L&SWR again to gain running rights through to Wimbledon. This undertaking was completed in 1889. The branch from the Richmond route to Ealing Broadway was opened in 1879 and this completed what we know as the modern District Line as far as West London was concerned.

One line that will feature again in our story that was also build during this period was an independently sponsored route from the District's Ealing extension which branched off between Acton and South Ealing to head out to the village of Hounslow. It was opened first to a station at Hounslow Town on 1 May 1883 and then extended in July 1884 to Hounslow Barracks. This extension rendered the short stub to the original Hounslow Town station obsolete and that section was closed in 1886 and all services on the branch were run directly to Hounslow Barracks. From the outset the locomotives, stock and crews were provided by and operated by the District, Before leaving the early steam years and the construction of the original underground mention needs to be made of two lines that were built and would only later come to prominence. The first was a link from the London, Chatham & Dover Railway at

A steam service at West Brompton – this is a posed photograph dated 1876.

Blackfriars, through a tunnel under Snow Hill and linking into the Metropolitan at Farringdon. This prompted the Metropolitan to add an additional pair of tracks from King's Cross to Moorgate to cope with the extra traffic from this connection and made at King's Cross to the Great Northern Railway. The Metropolitan connected with another main line company, the Great Eastern Railway, with a junction at Liverpool Street in 1875, although this connection generated very little traffic and fell out of use within decades. The same powers that enabled the completion of the Inner Circle line also obliged both the Metropolitan and the District to continue east to Whitechapel, which was reached on the same day the Inner Circle was opened. Here a connection was made to the East London Railway that ran from Shoreditch, through Whitechapel (at a lower level than the District station, although there a spur was provided for a physical connection between the two) and onward south of the Thames to both New Cross, where a connection was made with the South Eastern Railway, and New Cross Gate where it met up with the London, Brighton & South Coast Railway. It was this line that incorporated a remarkable feat of engineering that would be the inspiration for the next chapter of construction of the railways under London; the Thames Tunnel, but more of that later.

So it was that by 1884 London had a network of railways originating under the streets of the city and feeding out to various suburbs. It is worth noting that at the time of the railway's construction many of these places were little more than villages.

A Putney Bridge service from Mansion House reaches its final destination.

Hammersmith, Hounslow and Richmond, for example, were a long way from becoming the large districts they are now, but with the arrival of the railway that growth would be realised very quickly as the trains made it possible for many to live away from the squalor of central London and move out to these new fashionable districts. Commuting was on the rise.

The new railways, built against a backdrop of fierce competition, bitterness and rivalry, had many common features. They encircled London, but only the part that was on the north side of the Thames, with the District and East London lines being the only ones that reached south of the river. They were all built to take the full size trains as used by the main line companies which operated exclusively above ground and consequently they were all worked by steam locomotives hauling carriages lit by gas lamps. It was this combination of factors that threatened to be their undoing and one the underground railways needed to find a solution to prevent their passengers abandoning the increasingly sulphurous conditions underground in favour of the open air of the trams and horse buses. The early underground had focused on the traffic running from East to West, it was still a railway-free area inside the boundary of the inner circle line and no company was catering for the traffic running from North to South across London. There was plenty of scope for such a venture if a way could be found to open up these routes, and that would only become possible once a revolutionary new way of constructing underground railways was realised.

This engraving from *The Illustrated London News* shows how the area of disruption caused by the cut-and-cover method extended outwards beyond the width of the tunnel itself. This is the section near King's Cross station. *(JC)*

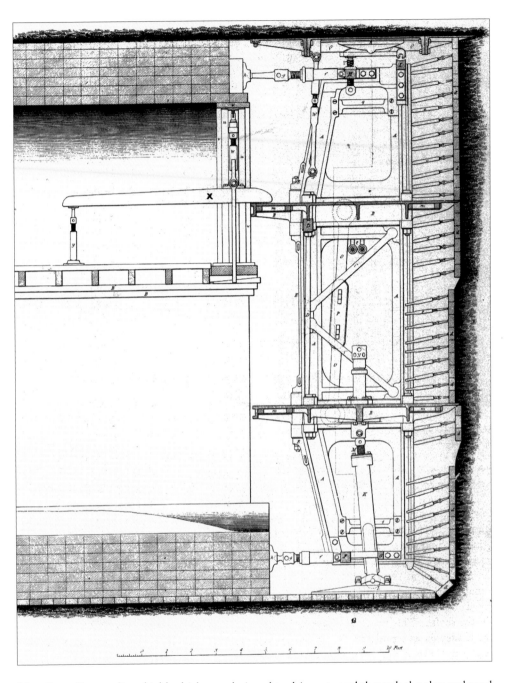

Marc Brunel's tunneling shield which was designed to drive a tunnel through the clay and sand beneath the Thames. *(JC)*

Chapter 2

An Elegant Pastry Cutter

The 'cut-and-cover' method of tunnelling had made underground railways a possibility for Victorian London, but this method came with some significant limitations. The method of construction meant that the railway line had to follow the path of either an existing or a new roadway, and where buildings were to be passed under the only way to do this was for the construction company to buy the building and demolish it. While the construction of a tunnel section was under way using this method the road above had to be closed to all traffic and this caused further disruption and congestion in London, something the underground railways were meant to relieve. What was needed was a way for a tunnel to be built, beneath both streets and buildings, with little or no disruption to the activities on the surface above. The story of how that was achieved is the story of three men, each of whom improved upon the work of the other and created the engineering prowess the world needed to create the first 'tube' railways.

The story begins long before the construction of the Metropolitan Railway. It was in 1823 that one of the boldest engineering projects ever undertaken was first proposed. The engineer Marc Brunel – the father of Isambard Kingdom Brunel – was proposing to build a tunnel underneath the River Thames from Rotherhithe to Wapping to ease the traffic congestion caused by horse-drawn vehicles going to and from the Surrey Commercial docks on the south side of the river. There had been two serious attempts to build just such a tunnel prior to Marc Brunel and both had met with failure due to difficulties working through the clay and sand, and the threat of flooding of the works leading many to conclude that building such a tunnel was impractical. Brunel did not subscribe to that theory and he devised a completely new method of tunneling. Previous projects had relied upon the experiences of coal and tin mining, which is done through solid rock strata. The Thames at this point had a bed of London clay and quicksand which could only be excavated using Brunel's new invention, the tunnelling shield. This was a giant frame with 36 individual sections in three rows of 12, in each of which worked a team of labourers digging out the earth. Wooden boards were removed one at a time to minimise the area of excavation exposed at any one time. The shield kept the shape of the hole they were digging intact and prevented the top of the roof of the workings from collapsing in on them. As the earth was removed a lining of bricks was constructed behind the shield to form the shape of the tunnel. The shield was then jacked forward and the whole process started again until it reached the end of the section to be dug. At each end of the tunnel a vertical access shaft was dug to lower the shield into position and supply the tunnelling team with both materials and a source of fresh air.

Investors in Brunel's Thames Tunnel were convinced that the idea would work and the capital was raised to commence work in 1825. Once completed, the tunnel would link the expanding dock areas on both banks of the Thames and provide a route for the conveyance of goods that would remove the need to travel either via London or boat to get from one side of the river to the other. It is important to note that when envisaged this tunnel was not intended for railway use as there were no railways in London at this time, the first of them being another decade away. Brunel planned a system of roads and access ramps that would allow horse-drawn vehicles to access the tunnel and pass safely under the Thames. When Marc Brunel's health began to fail it was his son, Isambard Kingdom Brunel, who was appointed as resident engineer in 1926 at the age of only twenty.

The excavation work was slow, with an average of ten feet a week achieved, and the scheme encountered many problems. The works flooded on numerous occasions, pockets of gas were frequently encountered and some workers lost their lives in accidents. Soon the money began to run out and 1828 work on the tunnel was suspended following a major flooding of the works. It was not until 1835 that it resumed, thanks to a loan from the Treasury. Conditions within the tunnel were apalling, floods and gas continued to blight the project and there were many who speculated that it would never be completed. Finally, in November 1841, the tunnel reached the north side of the Thames. There was no longer the finance to put in place the access roadways and goods and the tunnel was opened as a pedestrian thoroughfare on 25 March 1843. It had cost over £600,000 to build. The Thames Tunnel quickly established itself as a major tourist attraction with millions of visitors paying the penny toll for the then unique experience of walking under the river.

The tunnel was eventually sold to the East London Railway Company who intended to use it as part of their proposed line from Liverpool Street to New Cross Gate. The conversion of the tunnel for its new role and the construction of the railway was completed for the first train to run through it on 7 December 1869. The tunnel remains in use today as part of the London Overground network and is a Grade 2 listed structure.

Our next tunneller was Peter William Barlow, born in 1809. He was a civil engineer who came from a family of engineering pedigree. His father was a professor of mathematics and engineering and his younger brother was a civil engineer who would had found fame as the consulting engineer for both St Pancras station and the Clifton Suspension Bridge. Peter Barlow was also accomplished in bridge construction and was the designer of the Lambeth Bridge over the Thames. It was while sinking the cylinders for this bridge's piers that he realised that the cylinder used for cutting into the clay was akin to a pastry cutter and if the design could be turned through 90 degrees then it could be used to bore a circular tunnel. A circular tunnel would be more robust than Marc Brunel's rectangular one and by lining the tunnel wall with wrought iron segments instead of bricks it would be stronger still, with this circular lining creating a permanent tube. The gap left after the shield was driven forward between the tube and

The Thames Tunnel is opened for pedestrians.

Photographed in 2005, the twin entrances to the tunnel are still visible from the Wapping platforms. Note how the tunnel dips down towards the middle, a feature not shown in most contemporary images. *(JC)*

the tunnel wall could be filled with liquid cement to set the tunnel lining segments in place. Barlow patented his tunnelling shield idea in 1864 and was soon advocating its use in the construction of a system of underground roadways of 8-foot diameter under London. Barlow would get the chance to prove his tunnelling method for real with the construction of London's second underground river crossing.

In 1868 a company was formed to construct a tunnel from near London Bridge station, under the river to a site near Tower Hill, a distance of just over 400 metres. The Barlow tunnelling shield method of construction was used and the finished tunnel was a little under six feet eight inches wide. The Barlow method was far simpler than that used by Brunel and progress was rapid. This was also due to the fact that not only was Barlow's tunnel a lot narrower than Brunel's but also because he dug his tunnel deeper than the Thames Tunnel and only had to contend with the soft clay rather than the sand and gravel that plagued Brunel's venture. The tunnel took only ten months to dig and was ready to be fitted out from December 1869. Barlow had the tunnel equipped with a 2-foot 6-inch gauge railway along its length. To power the single carriage a cable worked by a stationary steam engine was fitted below the centre of the track a system similar to a claw would grab the moving cable and thus the carriage would be hauled through the tunnel. It would then release its grip at the other side and be slowed to a stop by hand brakes on the vehicle. The carriage had seating for twelve passengers and even offered the choice of first or second class. Lighting was provided by gas.

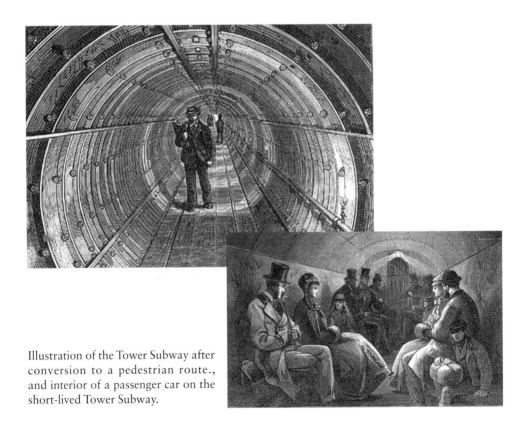

Illustration of the Tower Subway after conversion to a pedestrian route., and interior of a passenger car on the short-lived Tower Subway.

The Tower Subway, as it was known, opened to traffic on 2 August 1870 and can truly claim to be London's first tube railway. However, it was not the success Barlow had hoped for. The cable haulage equipment was temperamental and the limited space for passengers meant that the railway struggled to cover its operating costs. It closed in December 1870, the rails were covered over and the tunnel was converted to a pedestrian subway much like the Thames Tunnel had been. It remained open in this guise until 1898; the opening of Tower Bridge in 1894 had made the tunnel redundant. It was sold to the London Hydraulic Power Company who used it to run their hydraulic mains cables through, and in later years it was converted to carry mains water pipes and it continues in this guise today as well as providing a route for telecommunications cables. It has been sealed off from public view for well over eleven decades.

Peter Barlow was convinced that cable cars under London was the way forward and attempted to promote the construction of a larger tube railway from the City of London to Southwark, but when the Tower Subway proved financially nonviable at the end of 1870 he failed to raise the funds and it would be nearly another two decades before others took his vision forward. Barlow died in May 1885, thus never living to see his invention become the basis for a transport revolution. The baton had been passed to the man whom had been both Barlow's pupil and his on-site engineer for the Tower Subway; James Henry Greathead.

Workmen pass materials through the pressure airlock of the Waterloo & City tunnel.

Two images of the working conditions inside a tunneling shield.

Greathead was born in South Africa to English parents in 1844. He came to England in 1859 to complete his education and made his residency here permanent from 1864 and served a three year pupillage under Peter Barlow. After completing this he spent some time working with Barlow's younger brother William on the Midland Railway. He went back to work with Barlow senior when the work on the Tower Subway commenced. Greathead took a keen interest in the shield tunnelling system which Barlow had patented and went on to patent many improvements to the system, including the use of working in compressed air and using hydraulic jacks to move the shield forward. He worked on a shield that would bore a larger diameter tunnel, one that could accommodate standard gauge railway tracks and cars of reduced headroom. Greathead appreciated that steam locomotives would never be able to operate in his tube railways so he turned his attention to the alternatives that might be available. Since the limited period of operation of the Tower Subway in 1870 there had been advancements in the use of cable haulage in America.

A tight fit? A tube train is built to just fit inside the diameter of a tunnel. Note the completed iron segments.

Greathead had worked on several high profile railway projects, such as the Hammersmith and Richmond extensions to the District Railway, and also worked in Ireland briefly in 1884. He returned to London later that year to take up an appointment as principal engineer to the newly formed City of London & Southwark Subway Company. Greathead was the only man for the job, not only because of his knowledge of railway engineer and his unsurpassed experience of shield tunnelling, but also because he was the country's leading authority on cable haulage. All of this would be needed for a new venture to construct an underground railway from the City of London near Cannon Street south, under the Thames and terminating at the Elephant and Castle, a total distance of a mile and a quarter. The line was to be bored by shield tunnelling with two tunnels, one for trains in each direction. The trains would be worked using cables which were kept running continuously by stationary engines, three of which would be deployed along the route; similar to the method employed on the Tower Subway.

Construction began on driving the tunnels under the Thames in 1886. These tunnels had a diameter of 10 feet 2 inches, much larger than those of the Tower Subway. The company directors saw the potential of extending the line and obtained powers to build the line further south to Stockwell which would give it a total length of three miles. Curiously when the tunnelling commenced on the Stockwell section the tunnel diameter was increased to 10 feet 6 inches. The line was aiming to provide what the cut-and-cover underground railways had not delivered, a route into the City of London from the south. By 1888 construction was in an advanced state on both the line and stations and work had begun on the depot at Stockwell. The company made a re-evaluation of their proposed methods for working the line in the light of recent advances in technology. They felt that their line was an ambitious undertaking and deserved an equally ambitions new form of propulsion. They delivered a report to the shareholders in August that declared:

> After much careful investigation, and after obtaining the best technical and engineering advice, the directors have come to the conclusion that electrical force, conveyed by continuous conductors, offers the best solution to the difficulty.

London was set to have its first electric underground railway; history was in the making.

Chapter 3

The Potential of the Future

Electricity is a force of nature, and no one can lay claim to have invented it. The understanding of the nature of electricity and how it behaved had taken off during the early nineteenth century as the age of scientific enlightenment gathered pace. The science went from the study of static electric charges produced by rubbing rods of amber to understanding the nature of electrical current and ways in which it could be generated, stored and put to use in the service of man. Alessandro Volta had proved that electricity could be made by a chemical reaction caused when alternate layers of zinc and copper were used to sandwich paper or cloth that had been soaked in brine. This was the world's first battery and provided a means of making electricity available from an independent source that was derived from a static charge.

The next significant advancement was the discovery in 1819 of a relationship between electric current and magnetism. The Danish scientist Hans Christian Ørsted observed that current passed through a wire would influence the needle of a compass by exerting some invisible force. The discovery was further investigated by André Marie Ampère. But it would fall to a self-educated Londoner of more humble origins to enable the world to better understand the true nature of electromagnetism and what it could do for mankind. That man was Michael Faraday and he became one of the most influential scientists, not only of his day, but in history. Faraday was born in Newington Butts in 1791, his father was a blacksmith and young Michael received only a basic education. At the age of fourteen he got a position as an apprentice to a bookbinder and bookseller. It was during this seven year apprenticeship that Faraday had the chance to read a great many books. This coincided with a burgeoning interest in science. Faraday, once his working day was over, poured over volumes by the eminent minds of the day and fed his curiosity. After finishing his apprenticeship he committed himself to a career in science and worked as an assistant to Sir Humphrey Davy and subsequently worked at the Royal Institution. It was shortly after the discovery of electromagnetism that Faraday built his 'homopolar' motor, whereby an electric current caused a wire to rotate around a magnetic core in a bath of mercury. It was this experiment that laid the foundations for the electric motor and provided the means by which electric power could be turned in motion. In 1831 Faraday moved the science of electromagnetism on further with his work on electrical induction. Through a series of experiments Faraday was able to prove that electricity could be produced by motion and thus the way was set for the development of the dynamo and generator,

The Blacksmith's son, Michael Faraday.

Below: An illustration of the experiment whereby Faraday produced motion from an electric current and led to the development of the electric motor.

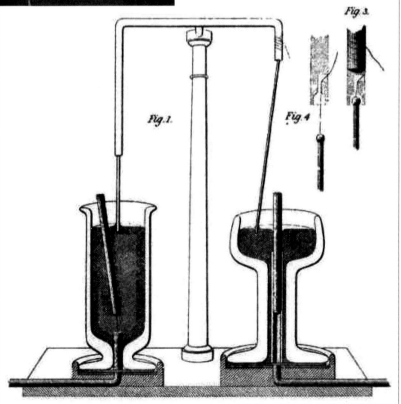

thus freeing up the dependence on batteries to supply electricity and allowing it to be produced in greater quantities as demand dictated.

The science of electromagnetism made massive strides as the nineteenth century progressed, with new ideas and enhancements developed from the work of Faraday made by a number of notable scientists and researchers. The development of electric motors slowly advanced as scientists sought to not only increase the size and power of the motors but also to find uses for them. One person working in this field was a Scotsman from Aberdeen by the name of Robert Davidson. He had trained as a chemist and made a successful business in the production of synthetic yeast for the baking and brewing industries. This gave him time to devote to his hobby of electromagnetism. He designed his own chemical batteries to provide power and, being a practical man, was enthusiastic about the potential of electromagnetism to drive machinery. By 1839 he had designed a printing press, a turning lathe and a four-wheeled car that all used Davidson's batteries and rudimentary electric motor. Davidson decided to demonstrate his inventions to the public and arranged an exhibition of his work, first of all in Aberdeen and subsequently in Edinburgh. He converted his car to run on a circular wooden track for the exhibition and even printed the handbills advertising the show on his electrically driven printing press. Davidson had such faith in the opportunities that electromagnetism offered that he had his eye on a bigger and more ambitious scheme. He approached the directors of the Edinburgh & Glasgow Railway for their support in building an electromagnetic locomotive. Railways were being built across Britain in the 1840s and they were all powered by coal-hungry steam engines. Davidson aimed to convince the new railway company that electric locomotives were a viable option. He even obtained the endorsement of the Royal Scottish Society for Arts in his ventures and they made him a £15 grant. He built a full size locomotive which was described as being 16 feet long and powered by Davidson's batteries. It was trialled on a section of the Edinburgh to Glasgow line in 1842 and was thus the world's first electrically powered railway locomotive. This was its only claim to fame as the loco only managed to achieve a speed of 4 mph and as the batteries were not rechargeable it was more expensive to operate than a steam loco. The directors were not sufficiently impressed to asked Davidson to take the concept further. The loco was reported as being destroyed whilst stored in the engine house at Perth, allegedly by steam loco enginemen who saw it as a threat to their livelihoods; word had obviously not yet reached them of its shortcomings. Davidson did not bother to have the loco repaired, perhaps he was satisfied with the fact he had simply built and operated a world first.

Electric railway traction would not advance again until 1879 when the German engineer Werner von Siemens demonstrated a small electrical locomotive at the Berlin Exposition. His design differed from Davidson's in that the power to drive the motors was supplied from an outboard dynamo and was fed to the locomotive through a conductor rail. The loco was brought to England in 1881 and was demonstrated at the Crystal Palace. Siemen's system was a portable demonstration installation but it marked the start of the period which saw the introduction of the world's first permanent electric railways and tramways. The dynamo had become a viable option for electricity generation thanks to the work of Siemens and Gramme and the provision of outboard

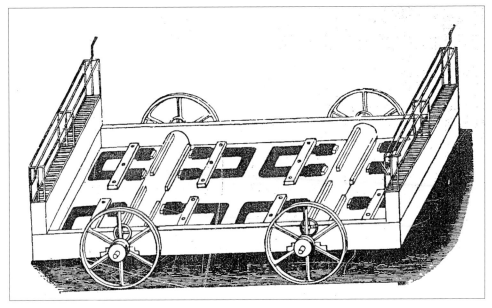

Above: Diagramtic representation from 1842 showing the arrangement of motors on Davidson's locomotive.

Right: Robert Davidson in later life.

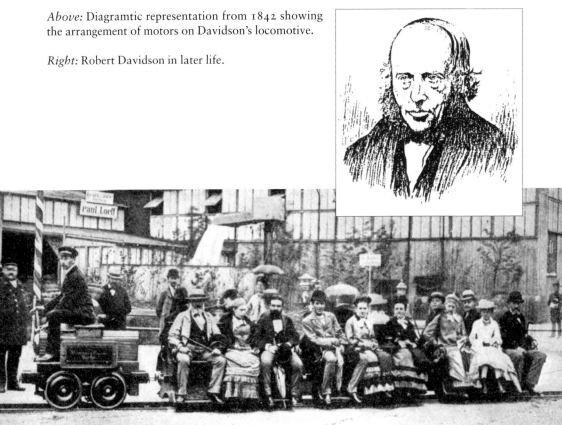

Siemens' electric demonstration line at the Berlin Exhibition, 1879.

A close up of the 1879 locomotive built by Siemens.

power was the breakthrough that was needed to make electric rail traction a possibility. Britain's first such line was built along the sea front at Brighton and opened on the August bank holiday of 1883. It was the brainchild of Brighton resident and engineer Magnus Volk. Like Siemen's installation Volk used a small generating station to supply current to the rails that was collected by the little four wheeled tram cars. The line was an immediate success and was extended beyond its initial quarter mile length to become over two miles long. It is still operating today. Other electric railways and tramways appeared in Ireland and Blackpool and thus the scene was set for London to have its own electric railway.

It was almost as if the development of the electric train and the shield tunnelling system had occurred at the same time by design. The steam locomotive had serious limitations underground, as the sulphurous stations of the District and Metropolitan were testimony to. Cable haulage was never a serious contender for fast frequent rail traffic once electricity became viable. Indeed the best speed the City of London & Southwark Subway estimated to be achievable by cable was 14 mph, in their report of 1888 the directors confirmed their belief that electric working would offer not only a higher average speed but also more flexibility in shunting and the option to 'operate in something more akin to normal railway conditions'. In opting to build a tube railway the company was already embarking on a leap of faith in a largely untested technology. By then adopting the use of electricity they was leaping even further into the unknown.

C&SLR locomotive No.1.

Chapter 4

City & South London Railway

The first electric train ran under London's streets in December 1889. It was comprised of a small electric locomotive hauling two carriages, using the first deliveries of the locomotives and stock for the new line, and was run for testing and training purposes only. The power was supplied by a temporary generating station at Borough. The construction of the line had progressed well and despite some tunnelling difficulties at Stockwell, due to hitting a bed of wet gravel, the line was largely complete by early 1890. All that remained was the fitting out of the station, the new depot and the railway's own power station at Stockwell. The latter was necessary as there was no national grid at the time and the railway would consume a lot of electricity, not only for running the trains but also for lighting the stations. (All the stations had lifts from the platforms to street level but these were hydraulically powered.) The power station was initially fitted with three 450 hp steam engines fed from Lancashire boilers. These engines drove generators that supplied the 500 volt DC supply needed for traction. The live rail was position in the centre of the track on glass insulators and the running rails would serve as the negative returns. The company was brimming with confidence after the success of the trials and seeing the line nearing completion. They placed a Bill before Parliament to authorise an extension of the line further south from Stockwell to Clapham and allowing the name of the company be changed to the City & South London Railway to reflect the change in the nature of the operation. By July 1890 a train had traversed the entire length of the line and the railway was readied for its grand opening. The date set for this was 4 November 1890 and the guest of honour was none other than Edward, Prince of Wales (the future King Edward VII); he was accompanied by his eldest son the Duke of Clarence to make it a doubly royal affair. The party began at the line's northern terminus at King William Street where they descended by lift to the station where a ceremonial switch-on of the line was performed. The party then made their way by train to Stockwell for a luncheon after inspecting the new works along the route. This, of course, was only the ceremonial opening, the inspection that allowed the City & South London to open its doors to the fare paying public happened later that same day when the Board of Trade inspector, Major-General Hutchinson, gave the railway the authority to commence public operation. The company held off from doing so for a further six weeks until Thursday, 18 December 1890, to allow time to iron out any last minute hitches, the commissioning of the locomotives, rolling stock and station installation and to complete training for the staff who would run them.

An original C&SLR train of padded cell coaches.

The completed line ran from a northern terminus at King William Street in the City of London close to the site of the Monument to the Great Fire of London. It then ran through twin tunnels under the River Thames passing under London Bridge station where there was no C&SLR station at the opening of the line due to the lack of an agreement with the London, Brighton & South Coast Railway. The first intermediate station was at Borough, then Elephant & Castle, Kennington, Oval and on to the southern terminus at Stockwell. The intermediate stations had island platforms. The tunnel for these had been bored to a much enlarged diameter than the two running lines and was lined with brick.

The trains that operated the line were comprised of three coaches, with open platforms between them and gates, like on an old style of lift, which an attendant (or gateman) would open and close to allow to board an alight. The carriages had longitudinal benches running their length that gave a total seating capacity of thirty-two. The most unusual feature of the coaches was the windows on the body side which were nothing more than narrow slits. The designers had figured that as no one would want to look out of the window on a railway that ran entirely in a tunnel they needed only the minimum of glass. This feature and the upholstered interior earned the carriages the nickname of 'padded cells'. All thirty of the original carriages were built by the Ashbury Carriage & Iron Company. The locomotives that hauled them were four-wheeled, fourteen of them had built by Matther & Platt of Manchester who had also supplied the generators for the power station. The loco's appearance when seen from the front is best described as two upright pianos placed back to back. The cab ran the length of the centre line and contained the driving power controls, automatic air and handbrake controls. Each loco was crewed by both a driver and driver assistant. The electric switch gear was mounted under the loco body. The air reservoirs to feed the automatic air brake were mounted inside the body sides and were replenished at Stockwell as the loco did not have its own air compressor. The motors were known as the gearless type as the armature was mounted directly on the axle with the field coils in a case surrounding it. Many early electric traction units featured this form of motor until it was found that a separate armature driving the axle through a gearbox produced far more torque and prolonged the life of the motor.

The C&SLR had been built with none of the large scale disruption to London that the cut-and-cover method of tunnelling had brought, but the different style of construction of the line had not earned the company an exemption from being required to purchase any buildings that the line passed under, and as such the route largely followed that of existing roads. The C&SLR was very much a pioneer and the existing legislative powers had not been able to distinguish from the brutal construction method of the earlier underground railways to the shield tunnelling system to make allowances for the obvious advantages the latter would bring.

A total of 10, 000 people were recorded as using King William Street station alone

Illustration of the original King William Street terminus of the C&SLR.

Gearless motor, the armature is wrapped round the axle.

A geared motor; the case contains the motor, which drives the axle through the gearbox visible inside the wheel furthest from the camera.

The C&SLR power house at Stockwell.

on the opening day of service, many of whom were attracted to the novelty of travelling on a train under the river and the streets; something millions do as an unattractive everyday event nowadays was a completely new adventure back then. The service settled down to an average of 15,000 passenger using the train on weekdays, with a five minute interval maintained between trains. A Sunday service was introduced in April 1891. All journeys on the line were charged at a flat fare of 2d.

As the power station at Stockwell was struggled to supply sufficient power for the demands of the line a fourth engine and generator set was added to boost output. The service was popular and this exposed the shortcomings in its layout. The principle one was the northern terminus at King William Street. It was reached by a steeply inclined and curved tunnel under the Thames and the small locos struggled with the weight of their loaded train when negotiating this. The station layout was a single line with a platform either side, nominally one side for alighting passengers and the other for boarding. This meant that the train had very little time to detach the inward locomotive and bring the fresh locomotive to haul the train south again out from a siding and attach it to the train. The solution to this was to re-model the station with two tracks on either side of an island platform. This provided some relief to the marshalling of trains as it allowed two trains to be in the station at a time giving longer turnarounds. The station was still overcrowded and the company felt that it was in the wrong location altogether. A Bill was put before Parliament in 1891 allowing for the construction of a new pair of tunnels from Borough, incorporating a station at London Bridge, with interchange to the South Eastern Railway, then continuing under the river to Bank and Moorgate, where it would have interchange with the Metropolitan

Railway. The northern extension would terminate at the Angel in Islington. The bill took two years to be passed. Once it had been approved the C&SLR had the authority to extend on both ends of its line, although they did not start work on either straight away as there was now fierce competition for capital to construct new 'tube' railways. The C&SLR had proved that deep level underground railways were not only viable to construct but also, with the introduction of electric traction, they were commercially viable to operate. Like the Metropolitan thirty years earlier, their success attracted the attention of others and many similar schemes were being proposed. London was on the verge of a period of tube railway mania.

An illustration produced for *The Illustrated London News* at the time of the opening of the C&SLR. It is not strictly to scale and the station appears roomier and better lit than was the case.

Chapter 5

The Early Tubes

The C&SLR had provided the pre-cursor for a number of schemes to build tube railways under London's streets, not all of these came to fruition and those that did took several years to gain Parliamentary approval, raise the necessary finance and get the line built and equipped. The construction of the network of tube lines that crossed the open space inside the boundary marked by the route of the inner circle would take decades.

London had to wait a further eight years for the opening of its second electric underground railway. The Waterloo & City Railway (W&C) was supported by the might of a main line company, the London & South Western Railway. Their terminus was on the southern side of the Thames and did not afford very easy access to the commercial district in the City of London, and it was estimated that as many as 50, 000 people arrived at Waterloo bound for the City each weekday. The L&SWR, and others, saw the obvious advantage of a link direct to the city and proposals for building an underground link had been seriously pursued in the 1860s with the intention of powering the underground trams with pneumatic pressure. That scheme failed to attract support, possibly due to a lack of confidence in the untested means of propulsion. In 1891 a nominally independent company, supported by the L&SWR sought Parliamentary approval for the construction of an underground line from the

CLR coaches at their Wood Lane depot.

W&C original train.

Interior of a W&C train.

A broadside view of an original condition CLR locomotive.

Interior of the original CLR cars.

Above and below: The original CLR trains on trial.

L&SWR terminus at Waterloo for a distance of just over a mile and a half to Bank station in the City of London with no intermediate stations. After two years spent overcoming numerous objections Parliament gave their approval and work on the line commenced in 1894.

The construction was achieved mainly using Greathead's shield tunnelling system with Greathead himself acted as consulting engineer to the project. (There was a short section at the Waterloo end that had to be excavated using the cut-and-cover method.) The railway had its own power station at Waterloo to supply not only traction power but also station lighting. A lift to transfer coal wagons from the high level sidings of the L&SWR terminus to the W&C was provided and this was also the means for delivering the new rolling stock used on the line and it was also used when the stock had to be sent away for overhaul. Like the C&SLR the W&C used a third rail system at 500 volts DC with the live rail placed between the two running rails.

The line opened in 1898 with trains formed of four coaches; the two intermediate ones were trailer cars while the outer ones had a driving cab and carried all the electrical equipment. Through a system of heavy duty cables the motors on both the front and rear cars were controlled by the driver at the front simultaneously. This arrangement, similar to that used by the trains of the Liverpool Overhead Railway, was later regarded as a fire risk and not permitted on later tube railways but the W&C were not asked to modify their trains. Under the 1923 grouping of Britain's railways the line became part of the Southern Railway, and not London Transport, and SR built replacement stock in 1940. It was nationalised along with the rest of the SR in 1948 and became part of British Railways. New stock was provided by BR in 1993 and a year later the line finally passed into the ownership of London Underground Limited who operate it today. The line is best known by its nickname as 'the Drain'.

The next line to open was of a much greater length than the W&C and, like the Metropolitan and the District railways before, it was chasing the lucrative east to west traffic. However, unlike those earlier ventures it was going to use deep level tube construction to run right into the heart of central London, a factor in the line being named as the Central London Railway. It was ceremonially opened on 27 June 1900 by Edward, Prince of Wales, and opened to the public a few weeks later on 30 July. The line ran from Shepherd's Bush in West London to Bank station in the City. Trains of six or seven coaches of gate-ended clerestory stock, built mainly by the Ashbury Car Company, were hauled by steeple cab Bo-Bo electric locomotives that were designed and part built in America by General Electric Co. and shipped to London for final assembly in the CLR's sheds at Wood Lane. The locomotives had their own air compressors to feed the air brakes and each of the four axles was motoriseded using gearless type motors, the same as had been used on both the C&SLR and the W&C. The CLR had a power station built at Shepherd's Bush. The power had to be supplied from there to three separate sub-stations located at Notting Hill Gate, Marble Arch and Post Office (now St Paul's) stations to prevent the voltage from dropping as it travelled away from the source of generation. A single conductor rail was positioned between the running rails, as like the two previous lines but was energised at the slightly higher 550 volts DC.

The statue commemorating James Greathead can be found at Bank station, where three of the lines he engineered meet.

The CLR ran trains at frequent intervals, seven days a week, and like the C&SLR passengers were charged a flat fare of 2*d* for any journey regardless of distance, earning the line its nickname of the 'Tupenny Tube' which the company endorsed in its own promotional material. Like many of the early tube railways it had a twisted route over most of its length as it followed, for the most part, the layout of the roads overhead, the reason for this was to avoid paying compensation to landowners if the line had to be built below their property.

By 1900 the C&SLR had progressed both their northern and southern extensions. The line from Borough to Moorgate opened on 25 February. This meant the closure of the original terminus at King William Street and the abandonment of the original tunnels north of Borough under the Thames. On the third of June the Clapham extension opened. Two supply services for the opening of the extensions additional rolling stock and locomotives were ordered. The new carriages had full size windows this time and the new locomotives had enlarged air reservoirs giving them a more curvaceous side profile.

James Henry Greathead died on 21 October 1896 and never saw the opening of either the Waterloo & City or the Central London Railway, both of which he had consulted on. However his legacy is undisputed and he is commemorated with a statue (above ground) near to Bank station which the three early tube lines all serve.

As the twentieth century commenced London could boast three all-electric Tube lines, with yet more Tubes being proposed and competition growing with the trams above ground who were changing from horse-drawn services to electric traction too. This left the original underground lines of the District and Metropolitan railways looked decidedly jaded as they were still reliant on steam traction and suffered with the associated pollution. If they were to compete in the new century then a change was much needed.

The site of the original King William station is marked on the building that stands above it.

Chapter 6

Electrifying the Surface

There are two types of underground railway, the original ones built by the cut-and-cover method and those built by shield tunnelling. The Tube tunnels are much smaller in diameter than the surface ones and although the track gauge is the same for both at the British standard of 4 feet 8½ inches the clearance in tube tunnels is less and therefore the tube trains have a lower profile than their surface cousins. At the turn of the century two companies were running the surface lines in London – The Metropolitan Railway and the District Railway ran in tunnels through the busy parts of London from where open air lines took them to Wimbledon, Richmond, Ealing, Hounslow, in the case of the District and the Metropolitan running in the open air from Paddington to Hammersmith. They had extended their Baker Street to St Johns Wood line as far as Harrow in August 1880 and then onto Chesham in 1889 and from Rickmansworth to Verney Junction in 1897 where a connection was made with the Aylesbury & Buckinghamshire Railway which gave the Metropolitan the longest run of any underground company. The last extension by the Metropolitan was from Harrow to Uxbridge in 1904, the same year the District extended from Ealing to Rayners Lane to link up to the Uxbridge line (which had originally been their proposal). The District extended to the east too in a link up with the Whitechapel and Bow Railway which gave it a connection to the London, Tilbury & Southend Railway. The District ran a few services as far east as Upminster but mostly confined its eastern operations limit as far as East Ham.

The section that formed the Inner Circle was in tunnel and services continued to be worked by steam locomotives. Both companies used a similar type of 4-4-0 tank engine which was fitted with condensing apparatus whereby exhaust steam was re-routed back into the locomotive's water tanks rather than into the atmosphere. This was intended to keep the tunnels clear of smoke and steam but had a limited effect and it was not uncommon for the stations of both railways to have an unpleasant atmosphere most of the time.

With the advent of electric traction as a viable alternative there was now a way to relieve the inner circle of steam and provide a far more pleasant atmosphere to passengers who, by then, had the choice of going above ground on the new electric trams. The inner circle was operated jointly by both the District and the Metropolitan, but despite their close proximity in central London the two companies did not get along. On one matter they did agree and that was the need to electrify the tunnel sections of their respective lines. Both companies had sent delegations to the City & South London Railway to see electric traction in operation. Despite this common objective there was no co-operation on the system of electrification to adopt. The Metropolitan favoured an AC system using overhead trolley wires while the District preferred DC conductor rails. As services by both companies would have to share common tracks a standard system of electrification had to be agreed and to do this an adjudication committee was set up jointly by both companies. Both agreed to electrify the three quarter mile long section of line between Earls Court and High Street Kensington with DC current and build an experimental train to try the system out. The line was electrified with a positive conductor rail placed outside the track gauge and the negative return conductor rail was positioned on the outside of the other running rail. A temporary generating station was built at Earls Court supplying 600 volts DC to the conductor rail.

The train, six coaches of it, was built by Brown Marshall & Co. and featured four compartment trailers with a driving motor coach at each end. The electrical equipment was supplied by Siemens Brothers and was installed after delivery at the District Railway's sheds at Lille Bridge. Each motor coach had a gearless motor on each axle and the whole train was lit by electric lamps and fitted with air brakes, which was a new experience for the Metropolitan who still favoured the vacuum brake. The driver only had control of the leading set of motors when in motion and the rear car was un-powered due to the lack of a control cable running the length of the train. The

The Earls Court experimental train of 1900.

Putney Bridge station with newly installed conductor rails in 1905.

Original Metropolitan electric car showing gate end platform.

A Hammersmith & City Line unit.

The trial trip of the first Metropolitan electric train on 13 December 1904. Lord Aberconway, the chairman, is on the footplate.

first test runs were made on 9 December 1899 with the first fare-paying passengers carried by the experimental service on 21 May the following year. The experimental train remained in service until 6 November 1900 when the project was ended and the coaches were returned with fifty per cent going to each company. Some were absorbed into the steam-hauled fleets while the rest were sold on to other railways.

The adjudication committee ruled in favour of a low voltage DC system similar to that of the experiment with a conductor rail and insulated negative return rail, as had been trialled at Earls Court which was needed to eliminate earth leakage in the damp tunnel environment. The negative return rail would be installed in the centre of the track gauge with the positive on outside on either side, depending on suitability given the arrangements of point work for crossovers and the need to position the live conductor away from the edge of platform faces. Unlike the three previous underground railway schemes that had been built to be operated electrically from the outset this was a much larger undertaking and also a conversion from steam working. The work to construct the power stations and substations could be done away from the railway with no interference but the installation of the conductor rails and feeder cables would have to be done when the routes were closed to traffic, at night or by shutting sections during quieter weekend periods.

A District Line EMU of the type first delivered in 1903.

The District set about a policy of electrifying all their lines, not just those in tunnels – but this project was affected by other dealings in the District Railway boardroom (of which details will follow later). The Metropolitan confined their electrification works to their shortest routes from Baker Street to Harrow and Uxbridge, where electric trains began running in January 1905 and a full electric service commenced the following March. Aldgate to Earls Court (their portion of the inner circle) which went live on 1 July 1905 and finally the Hammersmith line from Paddington went over to electric operation on 6 November 1906. There were teething problems. The Metropolitan fleet of trains had to have their collector shoes modified and this resulted in some services on the inner circle being restored to steam operation for a few weeks in the summer.

One line that was not initially included in the proposals was the East London Railway which was independent of both the District and the Metropolitan. Upon electrification those two companies ceased to run any services after 1906 to New Cross or New Cross Gate and the line became operated by both the London Brighton & South Coast Railway and the South Eastern Railway. The East London Railway company were swayed to join the electric age after seeing the benefits it offered and the work to do so was undertaken in 1912. The four rail system was used and the ELR took their power for the electric traction supply from the UERL power station at Lots Road with the Metropolitan Railway providing the train service, which commenced on 31 March 1913.

One anomaly of the Metropolitan operation brought about by the change to electric traction was that of the through services from Verney Junction to Aldgate which were steam hauled for the most part of their journey and upon arrival at Harrow the locomotive was changed for one of the Metropolitan's fleet of new electric locomotives for the last leg of its journey, the opposite applied for the return northbound trip. These were to be the only locomotive-hauled passenger trains on the underground railways as technology had moved on to change not only the propulsion of the system but also the very make-up of the trains. London had joined the multiple unit age.

An original GN&C Railway EMU at the end of its working life in 1939.

Chapter 7

The Horseless Carriage

A more detailed look at the types of trains used on the underground lines appears later in this book but one development is so significant that it deserves to be examined in more detail and in the correct context. Up until 1903 the normal method of running trains was to have a locomotive hauling carriages, the same applied for both steam and electrically operated railways, although the latter offered the chance to further exploit the science of electricity and do away with the requirement for a separate locomotive. After all, a locomotive took up extra length on a train that passengers couldn't use and was not considered to be revenue earning. Also the need for a locomotive at the leading end of each train created extra track, staff and train movements around each terminus.

A train entering a terminus would need a second locomotive coupled to the rear upon arrival so that it could be hauled on its return trip. This necessitated not only the need to provide two locomotives but also two sets of crews for them. Also the additional locomotive needed somewhere to wait for the terminating train to arrive. Sidings took up extra space at terminals, required additional pointwork and signalling, and made the regulation of the movements in and out of the station more complicated.

Frank Julian Sprague, the father of electric traction.

Added to all that the time that a locomotive and crew spent in that siding waiting their next duty was time not earning the operator revenue. What was needed was a way to combine the motored portion of the train and the passenger portion with driving controls at each end and thus remove the need for the additional locomotives.

The earliest attempts at this were made in the last decade of the nineteenth century. The Liverpool Overhead Railway had coupled two powered carriages back to back with the motors controlled on both through a mass of high voltage cables linked to every notch on the driver's power controller in each cab. The system did work and was replicated on the Waterloo & City trains of 1898 but, as previously mentioned, the Board of Trade, which regulated safety on Britain's railways, did not like the greater fire risk associated with the high voltage cables running the length of the train. The City & South London Railway had experimented with a motored carriage train in 1895 but took the project no further. The Earls Court experimental train of 1899 had motored carriages but only the leading one was in use when the train was operated, the rear coach was a dead weight. The solution to this problem and one that would change the face of rail travel for everyone, came from an American in 1896, and quite by accident.

Frank Julian Sprague was born in Connecticut in 1857. After a formal education he took up a commission with the United States Navy where he was allowed to indulge his flair for invention. He developed an electric call bell system for use on a warship. He had a keen interest in the development of dynamos and attended the Paris Electrical Exhibition in 1881 and served on the judging panel of the Crystal Palace Exhibition of 1882. Sprague left the US Navy in 1883 and went to work for Thomas Edison, but just over a year later he left to set up his own company and set to work on an electric motor. Sprague developed a new way for tramcars to collect power from overhead trolley wires in 1887 and by 1888 had equipped a new street car network in Richmond, Virginia.

It was during his work with the control of electric elevators from 1892 to 1895 that Sprague's great breakthrough for electric railway traction came. Working on a system to streamline the control of elevators he developed a system that used low voltage control wires that operate a series of relays to speed up, slow down and stop the elevator. Sprague worked out that this same method of control could be applied to railway traction and thus any number of motor coaches, coupled together with a low voltage control line running the length of the train, would be under the control of a single driver simultaneously. This was the system the previous designs failed to master. The lower voltage required by the Sprague method of multiple unit control would get round the objections of the Board of Trade and allow all powered vehicles on the train formation to operate without the need to tow any dead loads.

Sprague's system was an immediate success and orders came in from all over the USA and beyond. One line that took up on this new technology was the Central London Railway who were forced to take action in relation to their early electric locomotives following complaints from landowners above the route of their line over the vibrations caused to properties when the trains passed underneath. At first the CLR tried to modify the locos with geared motors and new suspensions, and while this had

London's first EMU motor coach of 1903 is delivered to the Central London Railway.

a fair degree of success the CLR decided to replace the locos with multiple unit motor coaches making use of a technology developed by Sprague. Trains that employed this technology were known as electric multiple units (EMUs) and the CLR became the first railway in Britain to use them.

New motor coaches were constructed in 1903 and one was marshalled either end of a set of four original CLR loco-hauled trailer cars to form a six-car set. In due course some of the trailers were modified with the inclusion of a driving position at one end (known as a control trailer) so that trains could be split during off-peak periods and run as three-car sets. The layout of the passenger portion of the new motor coaches, which started just behind the leading bogie, was identical to that of the trailers being of saloon layout with a mixture of transverse and longitudinal seating, and a gate end platform provided at the inner end of the vehicle. The front portion of the vehicle was given over to the driving cab, behind which was an area as long as the leading bogie (of which both axles were motorised with geared motors). This contained all the electrical switching and control equipment, and while the passenger area was constructed and clad in timber the motor and cab end was clad in steel and gave the impression of being an amour plated head. Between 1926 and 1928 all the CLR units had their gate ends replaced with air operated sliding doors to bring them in line with more modern stock operating at that time. The units continued to faithfully serve the Central Line and were not finally withdrawn until July 1939.

One of the first lines to benefit from the outset of the multiple unit system was the newly constructed Great Northern & City Railway. This line was opened in February

1904 over a distance of 3½ miles from Finsbury Park (under the Great Northern Railway station) to Moorgate in the city of London. It was built entirely in tube tunnel but these tunnels had a diameter of 16 feet which permitted the use of surface gauge rolling stock. The line used multiple unit stock from the outset with the cars built in two batches by Brush of Loughborough and The Electric Tramway & Carriage Works of Preston. The second batch of cars were notable for being the first all-steel electric multiple unit cars built in Britain. The layout of all vehicles followed standard practice at the time with open saloon interior and gate end platforms. Both the positive and negative rails were placed outside the track gauge (as with the Earls Court experimental train) and this system was used until the original stock was withdrawn in 1939.

The electric multiple unit was now the new standard for any electric urban or suburban electric railway and all of the new stock ordered for the Metropolitan's and the District Railways' electrification was of this type. The earliest EMUs owed much to their American ancestry being of open saloon layout with clerestory roofs – they could have come straight out of a Wild West movie. This was a massive improvement on the previous standard of carriage provided on the surface lines which was a four-wheeled gas-lit compartment type coach that had little changed in sixty years. Electricity offered the travelling public not only electric lighting but also electric heating that could be kept at a regulated temperature. With the advent of the EMU the days of the locomotive-hauled train was numbered. It would not take long for them to disappear from the underground and within a century from their invention nearly every rail journey in Britain is made on a form of multiple unit train that owes its existence to Frank Sprague.

Newly-built EMU motor coaches for the GN&C Railway.

Chapter 8

The Yerkes Empire

Charles Tyson Yerkes was born in Chicago in 1837 and became a very wealthy man through brokerage and investments in tramways and urban elevated railways within that city. He came to London in 1900 backed with millions of pounds provided by US investors and international banks to invest in buying up urban railway schemes in the capital, both completed and part completed schemes. That same year he acquired the Charing Cross, Euston & Hampstead Railway (CCE&HR) and followed this in 1901 with the purchase of the District, Brompton & Piccadilly Railway, Great Northern & Strand Railway and the Metropolitan & District Railway. He completed his group of lines with the acquisition of the Baker Street & Waterloo Railway (BS&WR) in 1902.

Yerkes established a holding company for the management of the group of lines which in 1902 became known as the Underground Electric Railways of London Limited (UERL). It is worth noting that at the time the only railway within the group to be completed and open for business was the District Railway, still steam-hauled at the time of acquisition. It was with money from the UERL that the electrification of the District Railway was achieved. The development of the other lines within the UERL group was:

District, Brompton & Piccadilly, Great Northern & Strand Railways

The District, Brompton & Piccadilly Railway was authorised for construction in 1897 in two separate parts, the first was a deep level tube line from Earls Court to Mansion House and the second was a tube line from South Kensington to Piccadilly Circus. The Great Northern & Strand Railway was granted permission for construction in 1899 from Wood Green to Aldwych on the Strand by deep level tube line. Construction on either line had not started when Yerkes acquired them in 1901 due to problems raising the necessary capital, something the UERL group was able to provide. Yerkes gained approval to join the two projects together between Holborn and Piccadilly Circus and linked the western end of the DB&P from Earls Court to join with the District, while the South Kensington–Mansion House section of that scheme was dropped along with the Finsbury Park–Wood Green portion of the GN&S.

Kings Cross, Piccadilly Line, platform when completed in 1906.

The new look line was finished and opened for traffic between Finsbury Park and Hammersmith in December 1906 with the branch from Holborn to Aldwych opening in November the following Year.

Charing Cross, Euston & Hampstead Railway

When Yerkes bought this company in 1900 it had Parliamentary approved powers to build a tube line from a southern terminus under Charing Cross to Hampstead with a branch line from Camden Town to Kentish Town. Like the DB&P and GN&S schemes previously mentioned, the CXE&H was also having great difficulty in raising the capital to construct its proposed line, and as with the other schemes it was only when Yerkes took them over that construction could be funded.

In 1902, while construction was commencing, the UERL obtained powers to extend the proposed length of the Charing Cross–Hampstead line further north to Golders Green and the branch to Highgate (Archway). The completed railway was opened for business along its entire length on 22 June 1907.

Baker Street & Waterloo Railway

In 1893 this company gained approval to build a tube railway from Lower Marsh (Adjacent to Waterloo station) to Upper Baker Street. The company had great problems in attracting sufficient investment to finance to construction until the London & Globe Finance Company agreed to provide backing. Construction was commenced in 1898, by which time the powers to build the line had been revised to allow an extension beyond Baker Street to the new London terminus of the Great Central Railway at Marylebone. Further extensions were authorised in 1900; at the north end from Marylebone to Paddington, and at the south from Waterloo to Elephant & Castle.

Despite these outwardly affluent signs, matters went horribly wrong for the BS&W. The principle character behind the London & Globe Co., Whitaker Wright, was arrested for fraud after a number of his associated companies collapsed with substantial debts. In 1901 he was found guilty and sentenced to seven years imprisonment. However, before being taken down to start his sentence Wright was allowed a private meeting with his advisors and during this unsupervised meeting he obtained a cyanide capsule and used it to commit suicide and avoid the shame of going to prison. Wright's suicide and the ensuing scandal forced London & Globe into liquidation and as a result work on the partially complete BS&W slowed to a near halt.

Yerkes' UERL purchased the BS&W from the liquidators in March 1902 and as a result fresh capital became available for construction work to resume. Rapid progress was made and the first section to be opened to the public was that from Baker Street to Waterloo on 10 March 1906. The section from Waterloo to Elephant & Castle opened five months later, Baker Street to Marylebone opened in March 1907 and the final section from Marylebone to Edgware Road station opened three months after that.

Oxford Circus, Bakerloo Line, prior to opening.

The Bakerloo depot at London Road full of units between duties.

The UERL had decided to defer construction of the Edgware Road–Paddington section shortly after taking over the BS&W.

In 1910 the GNP&B was renamed the London Electric Railway and the BS&W became the LER Bakerloo Line (from 'BAKER' Street combined with Water'LOO'), the CCE&H became known simply as the 'Hampstead Line'.

Sadly the architect of this scheme, Charles Tyson Yerkes, never saw his ambition realised as he died of kidney failure on 29 December 1905 while on a business trip to New York. It is quite possible that without his intervention many of the lines we know today as part of the London Underground may never have been built as it was evident that the schemes were faltering and their futures were very uncertain. By bringing many competing schemes under the control of a single group Yerkes not only made new construction happen but brought about a standardisation and common purpose that laid the foundations for the integrated Underground we know today. It was only appropriate that even after Yerkes death the UERL continued to work to his vision and went on in 1913 the to obtain control of both the City & South London Railway and the Central London Railway, thus leaving the Metropolitan, Great Northern & City and Waterloo & City Railways as the only underground electric railways in London outside of its control. Thus was sown the seeds for the modern London Underground network.

In little over two decades central London had been criss-crossed by Tube and Underground railways all powered by electricity. Millions of people were conveyed to and from work every day from suburban districts that less than fifty years previously had been little more than villages. The commuter had been re-invented, as had the type of trains they travelled in.

Chapter 9

District Railway Electrification

Electrification of the District Railway became financially viable after the company was taken over by UERL and that company's American backers used the developing technology from their homeland to equip their new acquisition. A power station was built in Lots Road, Chelsea, to supply the whole railway at 600 volts DC. A new depot was built at Ealing Common and a brand new fleet of trains had to be ordered.

The District started a policy of classifying its EMUs with a letter of the alphabet, a policy still continued today on the London Underground surface lines, letter by letter here is a guide to their EMUs from 1903 to 1935.

A Stock

Following the Earls Court experiment the District set up a full scale trial of its intended widespread electrification equipment on the line between Mill Hill Park and South Harrow. To evaluate available EMU technology two seven-car trains were ordered from Brush Traction. Each train was formed of three motor coaches and four trailers with the formation of M-T-T-M-T-T-M. The general appearance of the cars was very much in keeping with American practice with flat-sided wooden bodies with clerestory roofs and gate end platforms. The motor coaches at the outer end had a luggage compartment behind the driving cab whilst the intermediate motor coaches had a driving position in a cupboard at each end which could be locked out of use when not needed. One feature that was unique to this stock was the provision of current collector shoegear on all bogies. The saloon of all vehicles had an addition set of hand operated sliding doors on each side in mid position to provide addition boarding/alighting positions to the gate ends.

The initial trials (available for general passenger traffic) took place from 23 June 1903 between Mill Hill Park and Park Royal, with the run being extended to South Harrow from five days later. Following the widespread introduction of electric working on the District Line the A stock were confined to working the shuttles from South Acton to Hounslow as they were incompatible with later builds. Some of the trailers were converted to control trailers to permit the operation of two-car sets. The units were withdrawn from service from this route in 1925.

B Stock train on test, and posed for the camera prior to introduction into service.

B, C, D & E Stock

The B stock was the original mass produced EMU for the commencement of full electric services on the District which started on 13 June 1905 on the Hounslow line and from Whitechapel to Ealing on 1 July 1905, the same day as the start of electric operation on the inner circle line. The section from Whitechapel to East Ham was electrified on 20 August 1905 and from East Ham to Barking on 1 April 1908. From that date the District stopped running beyond Barking. The electrification works for this section included the provision of two extra tracks to relieve congestion with the London, Tilbury & Southend Railway traffic.

420 vehicles of B stock were built to enable sixty seven-car trains to be made up. 280 of the vehicles were built in France by train builder Ateliers de Construction Du Nord with the remainder built in Britain by Brush and the Metropolitan Amalgamated Works. The style and train formation closely followed the A stock except for the replacement of the gate ends arrangement with sliding doors which were initially powered by compressed air, these proved troublesome in service and were subsequently altered to hand working. 192 of the vehicles were built as driving motor coaches with thirty-two control trailers and the remainder as plain trailers. The motor coaches had steel frames whilst the trailers were all timber in construction.

The C stock comprised of thirty-two motor coaches and twenty trailers built by Hurst Nelson in 1911 to the same basic pattern as the B stock though all vehicles had steel framework and hand operated doors from new. The D stock appeared a year later and was a batch of twenty-two motor coaches and eight trailers built by Metropolitan Amalgamated to the same pattern as the C stock. The first departure in styling came with the delivery in 1914 of the twenty-six motor coaches and four trailers that made up the E stock fleet as these featured elliptical rather than clerestory roofs. The B, C, D & E stock were all fully compatible with one another from new. Due to the joint operation nature of the Whitechapel to Barking section thirty-seven motor coaches and thirty-seven trailer coaches were owned (on paper at least) by the London, Tilbury

& Southend Railway although they were integrated into the whole District fleet and used wherever on the network they were needed. These cars had a cast ownership plate attached to the solebar.

F Stock

The arrival of the F stock during 1920/21 signalled a radical departure from not only previous District units but from all EMUs previously built in Britain. These Met-Cam built vehicles were made entirely from steel (which earned them the nickname 'Dreadnoughts') and featured elliptical roofs. They were designed with higher performance in mind as each axle of the motor coaches was powered and with a more express rated gear ratio. The fleet of 100 cars was made up of forty motor coaches, forty-eight trailers and twelve control trailers and they were run in eight-car formations made up of a five-car M-T-T-T-M and three-car CT-T-M which could be detached during off-peak periods. All vehicles had three pairs of hand operated sliding doors on each side. It can be said that these vehicles were the first electric units built in Britain that looked British, rather than American, in their outline. They had very distinctive oval shaped cab and body end windows. Electrically they were incompatible with earlier built stock but this worked in their favour as they were used as test-beds for new technology that was emerging and as such the whole fleet were equipped with electro pneumatic brakes between 1928–30 and had their doors converted to air operation in 1938. They were transferred to the Metropolitan and East London lines in 1951 and the last examples ran in 1963. Regrettably, nothing of this elegant and ground breaking class survives.

An F Stock of 1920.

G Stock motor car after conversion to Q Stock designation.

G Stock

These were a batch of fifty double-ended motor coaches built by Gloucester Carriage & Wagon Company in 1923. Their motor equipment was reclaimed from older B stock motor coaches that were converted to trailer cars (and reclassified as H stock). The saloon interior featured the usual mix of transverse and longitudinal seating. Two pairs of hand operated sliding doors were provided on each bodyside, the styling of the G stock marked the re-appearance of the clerestory roof that had not been a feature of the E and F stock.

K, L, M & N Stock

There were no designs designated H or I Stock so the next batch were 101 vehicles of the K type and were delivered from the Birmingham Railway Carriage & Wagon Company in 1927. They were all double-ended motor coaches like the G stock and differed little in internal layout from them, however their external styling was such as to give a far more rounded off appearance. L Stock was a fleet of eight motor coaches and thirty-seven trailers built along the same style as the K stock by the Union Construction Company in 1932. M Stock comprised of fourteen motor coaches and fourteen trailer coaches built in 1935 by the BRC&W Co. Also a clone of the K stock design and finally N Stock were twenty-six trailer cars built by Met-Cam in 1935 that also copied the K stock profile.

K Stock motor coach as built in 1927.

A mixed rake of new and old vehicles pictured at Acton in 1928.

L Stock motor car.

Interior of an L Stock trailer showing the first-class seating area.

Chapter 10

Early Tube Trains & Extensions

The stock for the three original lines opened by the UERL was built to the same basic style which itself followed the layout established by the 1903 built trains provided for the CLR, having saloon layout with gate end platform and the motor and switch gear compartment immediately behind the driving cab. The Bakerloo and Hampstead vehicles were built in Manchester by the American Car & Foundry Co. which purchased and equipped their works especially for the construction of these vehicles. The cars for use on the Piccadilly were built by two European manufacturers; The Hungarian Railway Carriage & Machinery Works in Raab, Hungary, and Les Ateliers de Construction in northern France. The units began working from the opening dates of the railways concerned. Originally envisaged to operate with a six car formation they were in fact used in anything from two car formations upward as traffic demanded, but there was never more than two motor coaches in a formation at any time. A number of cars were converted to air door operation during the 1920s but they were eventually displaced by later deliveries of 'Standard' stock. The last operational pair of motor coaches saw use on the Holborn –Aldwych shuttle service in the late 1940s.

The Bakerloo extended the short distance from Edgware Road to Paddington on 1 December 1913. The next planned an extension to Queens Park via Kilburn Park where there lay the opportunity to link up with the new suburban services of the London & North Western Railway. In 1914/15 twelve new motor coaches were built for this extension. They made two significant departures from the tried and trusted layout of cab/switch compartment/saloon/gate end of previous builds in that there was an additional passenger door located halfway along the saloon which featured an electric lock which the gateman operated prior to departure from any station. Secondly these cars were made entirely from steel which by this time had become a board of trade requirement for all new deep level tube stock. The extension opened to Kilburn Park on 31 January 1915 and to Queens Park on 11 February 1915.

The CLR had extended their western terminus into a giant loop around Wood Lane and opened it in 1908 with a new station to serve the White City Stadium. Their eastern extension was from Bank to Liverpool Street to provide interchange with the Great Eastern Railway, and the Inner Circle. That opened on 28 July 1912, both of these extensions required no additions to their fleet of 1903. They next obtained twenty-four new motor coaches for use on their Ealing extension in 1915. These followed the same style as the Bakerloo stock mentioned above but with the main difference

The gate ends of early Tube cars.

An exhibit by the Central London Railway of 1909 showing a motor car, signals and a section of tunnel.

of not having gate end platforms but an enclosed end vestibule with swing passenger door. Prior to entering service on the CLR these cars were loaned to the Bakerloo due to late delivery of their own additional stock. Once in service with the CLR they were found to be incompatible with the original 1903 motor coaches and thus had to be marshalled at one end of a train with a like motor coach at the other end. The completion of the Richmond extension works were heavily delayed by the outbreak of World War One and were suspended for the duration. The extension finally opened on 3 August 1920. The CLR were only responsible for the construction of the short section from Wood Lane to Wood Lane Junction where the connection with the GWR line was made. The route onward via East, North & West Acton stations was built by the GWR. The CLR trains shared Ealing Broadway terminus not only with the GWR but also the District Railway.

To work the services of Bakerloo over the LNWR line to Watford the UERL ordered a fleet of thirty-six motor coaches, twenty-four trailer cars and twelve control trailers.

A 1920-built Brush car in the early stages of construction, showing the raised area of the sole bar where the motor bogie fitted.

Interior of a completed 1920 UERL car.

UERL Standard Stock trailer car as built.

Original CLR Stock of 1903, converted to air-door operation.

Due to the outbreak of the First World War these were not delivered until 1920–22, although Bakerloo trains had started to appear as far north as Watford from 16 April 1917 using stock borrowed from other lines. The new trains were formed of a two- and a four-car set with the later having two trailers between two driving motor vehicles and the former being formed of a driving motor and control trailer car. The two car portion was detached from the formation in off-peak periods. The layout of the cars followed the practice set by the 1915 CLR cars with all doors of the swing type and provided at each end and in the middle of the passenger saloons. In order to obtain Board of Trade permission to operate with a driving motor car in the middle of the formation it was necessary to alter the layout of the switch compartment to make provision for a through walkway for use by passengers in an emergency. Although designed to UERL standards these units were jointly owned by the UERL and the LNWR. In service the units proved to be not as reliable as expected and slower than other stock of the era, most were withdrawn from Bakerloo service by 1930 but three three-car sets survived long after the bulk of the fleet was withdrawn under the ownership of the London Midland & Scottish Railway for use on the Watford–Rickmansworth and Watford–Croxley Green branches and remained on their books until scrapped in 1939.

Standard Stock and a Metropolitan unit side by side at Uxbridge in 1932, showing the obvious differences in loading gauge.

The first cars to be built with air operated sliding doors were twenty trailer and twenty control trailer vehicles built between 1919 and 1922 for use on the Piccadilly line where they operated with a batch of original French-built motor coaches that were modified with air operated sliding doors to match them. The cars were all built by Cammell Laird and featured saloon layout with entirely longitudinal seating. Four doors were provided on each side of the trailers, one at each end and two in the middle divided by a central pillar. The control trailers had the same arrangement but the door at the end adjacent to the driving cab was for use by the driver only. These cars remained in use until 1938.

UERL Standard Stock 1923–1934

During 1923–34 the UERL took delivery of a large number of driving motor, trailer and control trailer vehicles built to a standard design by four manufacturers; Met-Cam, Cammell Laird, the Birmingham Railway Carriage & Wagon Company and the Union Construction Company (A subsidiary of the UERL). Although there were a number of refinements made during deliveries of subsequent batches the vehicles are always referred to as the 'Standard Stock'. The layout drew inspiration from the air door trailers of 1919 except for the reappearance of some transverse seating and the pillar between the middle pair of doors was reduced in size on these units and eventually eliminated on later batches. Like all previous tube stock the standard stock featured a clerestory roof but it was more subtle.

The standard stock found use on all lines within the UERL group, but the lines themselves were anything but standard, having been built by various concerns. The plan was to link City and South London Railway to the Hampstead Railway at a junction just north of Euston. The problem was that the C&SLR had been built with tunnels that had a diameter of 10 feet 2 inches on the original section, and 10 feet 6 inches on the subsequent extensions, while the Hampstead line had tunnels of 11-foot 8-inch diameter. In order to have standard stock running on both the C&SLR had to be operated at a reduced level for eighteen months with Kennington and Borough stations closed for the duration of the works. The Stockwell power station had been closed a few years earlier in 1915 when the UERL had used their District power station at Lots Road to supply the line and the former site of this became a central depot for the works. The works were progressing well with limited operation supplemented by replacement buses, but on 27 November 1923 part of one of the tunnels collapsed and narrowly missed a train. The subsidence ruptured a gas main in the road above and caused a huge explosion. Remarkably nobody was injured by this but the C&SLR was closed until all tunnel enlargement work had been completed. Thus the last days of locomotive operation were brought to a premature end as the line re-opened with the connection to the Hampstead line and the new standard stock operational on 1 December 1924. The electrification equipment was now the standard four rail system too. On 13 September 1926 a southerly extension to the line from Clapham to Morden was opened. The two railways then became the Northern line, the C&SLR section became the 'City' branch and the Hampstead section the 'Charing Cross' branch.

The standard stock proved reliable and an effective people mover during a service life that lasted until the mid-1960s when the final cars were withdrawn. Among the innovations introduced on later batches was the introduction of electro-pneumatic braking which became standard on all subsequent tube and surface stock builds and was retrospectively built into earlier stock. After withdrawal from the London Underground a number of cars were sold to British Rail where they enjoyed a further twenty years of service on the Isle of Wight.

Interior of 1927 trailer 7469 as 1901, on 8 September 1975.

Chapter 11

Behold, Metroland

The Metropolitan Railway operated over the northern side of the Inner Circle from Aldgate where it ran trains to Aylesbury via Baker Street, Harrow-On-The-Hill and Rickmansworth, and also the branch lines from Paddington to Hammersmith, Harrow to Uxbridge and from Chalfont to Chesham. Under the direction of its Chairman, Sir Edward Watkin, the Metropolitan played a vital part in the plan he had conceived to transport passengers from Manchester to Dover and onward to the continent via a channel tunnel using the three railways under his control, namely the Great Central, the South Eastern and of course the Metropolitan. Grand plans indeed.

By the turn of the century the Metropolitan had to act to improve its service to the suburbs, which despite Watkins grand dreams was really the bread and butter traffic to the railway. Electrification of the Inner Circle (in co-operation with the District Railway) and the Hammersmith and City branch along with the main line to Harrow and the Uxbridge branch was completed during 1905/06. The Metropolitan employed EMUs which were like those early units of the District being American in outline with clerestory roofs, saloon interiors with gate end platforms, the later feature was not successful for the mainly open air MET and only the first batches had the feature which was soon modified to provide enclosed vestibule ends.

For the Metropolitan's longer distance services the need for steam traction continued on lines north of Harrow but for the journey from this point to and from the city steam was replaced. At first the Metropolitan converted its bogie stock to be hauled or propelled by a standard EMU motor coach as they had equipped all of their such vehicles with four traction motors and felt they would be adequately powered for the task. This proved not to be the case and the railway invested in a fleet of twenty Bo-Bo electric locomotives to haul its bogie coaches from Harrow to the City and back. The first ten of these locos arrived in 1906 and they had a tall central cab with an angled bonnet either side of it which housed the air compressor, traction and brake control equipment. The second batch of ten arrived a year later and these had a flat fronted box-like appearance. Also in 1906 the Metropolitan converted numbers of the former steam hauled bogie coaches into EMUs to provide cheap options to supplement the existing fleet. The company was not all about economy though. They recognised an opening for a premier level of service for their wealthiest clients and they became the first railway in Britain to offer an electrically hauled Pullman service when it provided one such car on certain commuter workings between Aldgate and Aylesbury.

Metropolitan electric service at Faringdon in 1950.

Metropolitan stock working an Inner Circle service.

Bogie steam-hauled stock converted to EMU use by the Metropolitan for their early electric services.

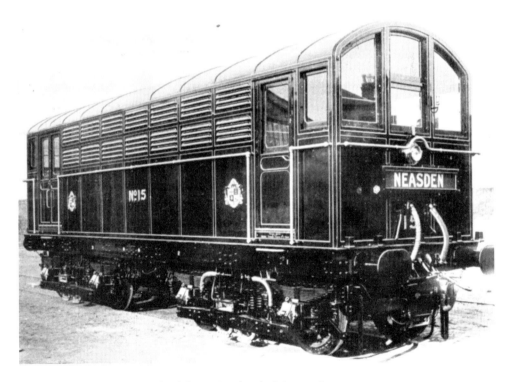

One of the ten electric locos built by B.T.H. for the Metropolitan.

Interior of a B.T.H. locomotive.

B.W.E. electric locomotive hauling a northbound Metropolitan service, which includes a Pullman car in its formation.

A train of MW Stock heading for Baker Street.

T Stock was the name given to the MW stock from 1931.

Still in use on special duties, Metropolitan Bo-Bo No. 12, *Sarah Siddon*s.

Electrification had proved popular with passengers and the numbers using the electric trains rose against those who had endured the underground steam service. Due to demand there was a requirement for new stock and the arrival of brand new elliptical roof saloon EMU stock for circle and Uxbridge line trains occurred either side of the First World War.

The Metropolitan had plans to electrify all the way from Harrow to Aylesbury in the early twenties and also to build a new branch line to Watford. Only the later was fully achieved, the branch from Moor Park to Watford opened on 2 November 1925 while the extension of the electrified lines got as far as it was ever to reach under Metropolitan Railway control when Rickmansworth went live three days after the opening of the Watford line. To work the Watford service new stock was required but in keeping with previous MET practice it was only part new. Twelve new motor coaches were delivered from Metro-Carriage in 1927 and these were roughly the same outline as the 1912-built MET bogie steam-hauled stock with all accommodation in compartments. The new motor coaches had each of their four axles motored and between the driving cab and luggage compartment was a compartment where the banks of electro-pneumatic contactors for the control of the motor equipment were housed. The trains ran with five converted steam-hauled compartment coaches marshalled between the motor coaches. Subsequent batches of motor coaches and purpose built compartment trailer coaches

Metropolitan Bo-Bo No. 10, *William Ewart Gladstone*. (JC)

were delivered in 1931 and 1932, the units were classified as T stock and remained in use on the Watford services until 1962. The Metropolitan had also taken delivery in 1922/23 of twenty new electric locomotives to replace the earlier locos of 1905 which were underpowered for the longer haul to Rickmansworth. The new locos were also Bo-Bo arrangement but had slimline bodies with a blunt V-shaped cab end. All of them were named after prominent historical or fictional figures with connection to the locality served by the railway such as Sherlock Holmes and Sir Ralph Verney. These locos hauled the Aylesbury trains of bogie stock from Aldgate as far as Rickmansworth where they were changed for steam traction for the remainder of the journey, one of the features of this service was the highly efficient changeover of locomotives that usually took as little as three minutes to achieve. Locomotive haulage ceased in 1961.

One of the last acts of the Metropolitan Railway was the building of the branch from Wembley Park to Stanmore which opened in December 1932, included with the programme to build this branch was the four tracking of the section of line from Wembley to Harrow.

The Metropolitan Railway owned large plots of land adjoining its main line and was free to sell these onto property developers to build new housing estates which were becoming needed as many sought to escape the cramped living in the heart of London. This became a win-win situation for the company as they not only benefited from the land sales but gained new patronage from those who moved in. The Metropolitan was keen to promote the virtues of residence in the suburban districts served by its trains and coined the phrase 'MetroLand' to describe them. Posters adorning stations and train interiors advising travellers to 'Come Live in MetroLand'.

The formation of the London Passenger Transport Board on 1 July 1933 resulted in the nationalisation of the Metropolitan, District and all other tube lines in the UERL group had little immediate effect on the operation and appearance of what became known as the Metropolitan Line. In due course new trains alterations to stations and services and extension of the electrification would come but even after all this the Metropolitan still retained a distinctive air all of its own.

Chapter 12

New Works

The formation of the London Passenger Transport Board (LPTB) on 1 July 1933 allowed for a more centralised approach to be taken in planning the future development of the Underground system in relation to the suburban lines of the mainline companies. Schemes were soon drawn up to allow the Tube to take over the running of various under-used lines operated by the LNER and integrate them with the existing network. Most of these schemes would never have got further than the discussion stage had it not been for a government initiative aimed at using public works as a means of tackling spiralling unemployment in the mid-1930s. The government offered to subsidise loan interest on capital borrowed to carry out major works in areas where unemployment was high. London was one such area and the LPTB seized upon the chance to obtain cheap capital funding for many of its expansion proposals put forward as the 1935-1940 New Works Programme.

The schemes affected most lines but in many cases these were limited to building new or renewing existing stations and infrastructure, however on the Bakerloo, Metropolitan, Central and Northern Lines far reaching alterations and expansion was planned; line by line the proposals and the end results are explained thus:

Piccadilly Line

The previous idea of extending from Finsbury Park to Wood Green was revived. There had been considerable local pressure to extend the line beyond Finsbury Park which had become something of a traffic bottleneck due to patrons changing from trains to buses and trams to reach the north east suburbs of Wood Green, Tottenham and Southgate. The New Works programme finally made the finance to achieve this possible and extended upon the original proposal with the new line going to a northern station at Cockfosters.

The line was constructed in tube tunnel for the first half of its length and emerged into the open air at Arnos Grove. The need to pass under a hill meant further tunnelling at Southgate before the last section to Cockfosters being in the open.

The Finsbury Park to Arnos Grove section opened on 19 September 1932 with the section from Arnos Grove to Oakwood opening for traffic on 13 March 1933. The last section from Oakwood to Cockfosters was opened shortly after on 31 July 1933.

Bakerloo Line

The two-track section of the Metropolitan between Baker Street and Finchley Road was a notorious bottleneck due to the high number of services running from the Metropolitan main and branch lines trying to gain access to Baker Street Station and the City, the three stations that were located in this section made the problem worse with trains taking longer than their booked station stop time causing delays to following services. Under the new works programme a scheme was authorised that would enable the construction of a twin tube line from a junction with the Bakerloo line just beyond Baker Street (tube station) and run virtually below the Metropolitan lines to emerge at Finchley Road from where the Bakerloo would continue with its tube trains to run onto Stanmore. A re-modelling of the junction at Wembley Park would ensure the Stanmore trains would no longer cross the path of the Metropolitan main line. At the same time the Bakerloo's existing tube level stations would be rebuilt to allow the running of seven car trains and a programme of re-signalling on all the affected routes.

Work began on the works in 1936 and continued apace, included in the scheme was the construction of a vast new rolling stock depot for both Bakerloo and Metropolitan use on the site of Neasden Works. A station on the new tube line was built below the Metropolitan's Swiss Cottage one and a further tube station was provided between the sites of the St John's Wood and Marlborough Road, both of which were closed when the new station (called St John's Wood) opened for business upon the start of the Bakerloo service to Stanmore which commenced on 2 November 1939. The platform extensions were delayed by World War Two and did not come into use until 1946.

Central Line

The UERL had made little alteration the original section of the CLR except for the closure of the Wood Lane power station in 1928 and the supply of the line from Lots Road. The LPTB scheme devised for the Central was for extensions both east and Wwest. To achieve the former a plan was devised to construct new tube lines from Liverpool Street to emerge onto LNER tracks just south of Leyton where the Central would take over the running of services onward to Loughton and with a new section of tube line to be built from Leytonstone to Newbury Park (including three new intermediate stations at Wanstead Park, Redbridge and Gants Hill) the Central would have a continuous loop round to Woodford via Fairlop and Hainault (where new car sheds would be built). In the west was a scheme to project a branch from the existing Central line west of North Acton station to West Ruislip station where a new stabling and servicing depot was to be constructed. These plans were added to in 1937 when the western extension was authorised beyond West Ruislip to Denham and the decision was made to extend the operation of electric services by the Central in the east to cover the Loughton to Ongar section and thus relieve the LNER of all service responsibility in that part of Essex.

Another major part of the scheme was the re-alignment of the original Central London tube tunnels to allow standard stock trains to be used on the four-rail principle as the Central still used the original track gauge centre positive rail system of 1903 and the extension of the stations in this area to accommodate eight-car trains. It was this later part of the plan that was the first to be completed, the first Standard stock units were run on 12 November 1938 with the last day of use of the remaining original Central London units of 1903 vintage taking place exactly eight months later.

Work on both the eastern and western extensions was delayed due to the war and during the conflict many of the semi-completed stations and sections of tube tunnel were used as air raid shelters, the incomplete depots and some of the sections of tunnel were turned over to the use of the War Department for munitions and machinery production.

After the end of hostilities work on the extensions resumed with the first section to open being that from Liverpool Street to Stratford on 3 December 1946, the next section from Stratford to Leytonstone came into use on 5 May the following year. The first section of the western extension from North Acton to Greenford saw its first passengers on 30 June the same year and before 1947 ended the sections of line from Leytonstone to Newbury Park and Woodford opened on 14 December. Empty stock working to the new Hainault depot came into being a few months ahead of the public opening of the tube service from Newbury Park to Hainault on 31 May 1948. On 21 November 1948 the last section of the western extension came into use with the opening of Greenford to West Ruislip – the proposed line to Denham had been dropped due to 'Green Belt' restrictions on housing developments in that area. The same day the lines from Woodford to Loughton and Hainault opened for business, the latter completing the Fairlop loop. Loughton to Epping went live from 25 September 1949. This left the single track line from Epping to Ongar as the last steam-worked section. There was much 'heel dragging' over whether to electrify this section; a decision not being made until 1956 when a light electrification which limited the number of tube trains permitted on the branch at any one time to two was authorised. The line went live and completed the Central new works programme on 18 November 1957

Northern Line

Like the Central line plan this one involved the taking over of lines previously operated by the LNER; and also like the Bakerloo scheme the one for the Northern line also took over track previously managed by the Metropolitan. In the end this tuned out to be the most controversial of the lot.

The Plan envisaged the taking over of the Metropolitan controlled former GN&C line from Moorgate to Finsbury Park and diverting it just north of Drayton Park to run into new surface height platforms next to Finsbury Park LNER station. From here the Northern would take over the line to Alexandra Palace via Highgate. Just north of Highgate the line would continue over LNER metals to High Barnet and a link into it would be made from the existing Archway terminus line of the Northern which would be extended via a new tube level Highgate station to join the High Barnet line just south of East Finchley station. The Northern would also take over the LNER single track line which branched off the High Barnet line and ran to Edgware where a connection would be built to join the existing Northern line to that destination. North from Edgware a brand new stretch of line was authorised to be constructed to Bushey Heath. Along this stretch between Bushey Heath and Elstree South a new depot (Aldenham) was planned.

The project got off to a good enough start with the line from Archway to East Finchley being opened on 3 July 1939. World War Two started at the same time but works that were well in hand were allowed to continue and the East Finchley to High Barnet section was one such project. It opened for business on 14 April 1940. The single track line from Finchley Central to Edgware had been closed to allow work to proceed on doubling the formation for use by the tube trains service of the Northern line. As the first station on the line from Finchley, Mill Hill East, served a barracks the Northern opened up this section of single line for a tube shuttle service to aid the war effort from 18 May 1941. All other works had ceased due to the conflict. The partially completed depot at Aldenham was requisitioned and used for the construction of Halifax bombers.

Upon the end of hostilities work resumed on the many uncompleted new works projects. The Central line ones were given priority over those of the Northern which were left in limbo. During this period the London Underground re-evaluated the need for the Northern line extensions. New Green Belt legislation put restrictions on residential development in the outer suburbs thus reducing the scope for the expected increases in traffic flows from the districts served by those lines. Finance was also restricted and much was needed to rebuild other parts of the system damaged during the war. In 1950 the Underground announce the abandonment of both the construction of the Edgware–Bushey Heath line and the completion of the Edgware–Finchley Central sections, the later would remain only as the single track shuttle to Mill Hill East. Hopes remained that the Drayton Park–Alexandra Palace section would be finished but it never happened, the scheme was withdrawn and the last steam trains ran by the LNER over the line on 5 May 1954 were the last passenger trains to run.

Many of the redundant sections remained in use for a few more years for freight traffic run by British Railways. The depot building at Aldenham was converted into a major bus works but the semi-completed stations, signal boxes and sub-stations built by the Underground were simply abandoned.

Chapter 13

New Works, New Trains

The period from 1935 is when EMU design in the UK came of age. The London Underground, being the largest user of electric multiple units in Britain, were at the forefront of this age of progression and designed units that set the standards which were benchmarks for the next thirty years and have influenced train design beyond that. The one man who can be charged with the greatest responsibility for this was the Underground's Chief Mechanical Engineer, W. S. Graff-Baker who took over the post in 1934. These are the trains that came into being during and immediately after his reign.

1935 Experimental Tube Stock

With the announcement of the New Works programme came the need to provide modern efficient units to provide the more demanding service. Graff-Baker's team set about designing the new age tube train and set themselves the target of improving a number of key areas. Firstly the equipment had to be mounted under the floor so as to leave all available space in the car bodies except for the driving cabs available for passenger seating. Secondly the traction motors would be smaller and more evenly distributed along the train length to make for better acceleration and, thirdly the electrical equipment must be the most modern and efficient then available.

To put possible solutions to these demands into practice twelve two-car units (marshalled into four six-car trains) were built in 1935 each featuring different equipment from various manufacturers. The first nine units were built with a streamlined cab end with a view to achieving higher speeds whilst the final three units had a flatter front end. All units featured under floor equipment and as a result a six-car unit had the same seating capacity as a seven-car train of 'Standard' stock. All units were extensively trialled with the flat front style of body decided upon as the best design (the streamlining was found to have no positive benefit) with the equipment supplied by Crompton Parkinson decreed as the standard for the production trains. All the streamlined units were stored during the Second World War and when hostilities ceased they were all converted to trailer cars to insert in new 1938 tube stock units. The flat fronted units lasted a number of years on odd duties.

Streamlined 1935 experimental unit.

Older stock, like this Bakerloo Line unit from the opening of the line found extra life in use on service duties. This vehicle was converted to a rail grinding car.

1938 Tube Stock

These units were the production stock built as a result of the experimental stock mentioned above and were nearly identical to the flat front design of the last three units. The type went on to become the most numerous and widely travelled tube trains ever built and in many ways were as iconic an image of London Transport as were Routemaster buses or the black cabs. The units were built in four and three car sets, a four car was formed of a driving motor at each end which had a driving cab and two motored axles with an un-powered trailer and a non-driving motor (NDM) coach in between, the NDM had two powered axles like the driving motors but had no driving controls. The compressors were fitted to the trailer and NDM coaches and motor generator sets to the driving motors. Three car units had the same vehicles except for the NDM which was omitted from the formation.

After initial teething problems which did not get ironed out until after the war the '38 stock settled down to provide the back bone of tube services. During their life span they worked on the Bakerloo, Northern, Piccadilly and East London Line and also on parts of the Central line. Withdrawals started in the 1970s but the type was found to be indispensable and the last sets remained in service up until 1986.

Eighteen of the driving motor coaches found a new lease of life on the Island Line service between Ryde and Shanklin on the Isle of Wight.

Flat-fronted 1938 unit.

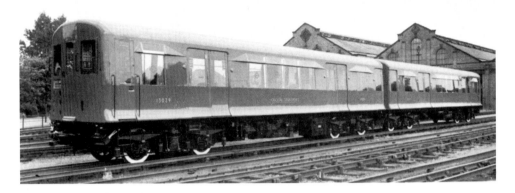

Brand new O Stock at Ealing Common Depot.

Interior of an O Stock car.

O and P Stock

Both the Metropolitan and Hammersmith & City lines were in need of new stock in the mid-1930s. So the opportunity was taken to push the available technology to the limits and produce a train that was fitting of the age. The result was the O and P stock types.

Both types were virtually identical with open saloon layout of each of their two driving motor coaches that initially made up each unit. A middle vehicle was added after a while to make them up to three car sets and this was a trailer car marshalled between the driving motor vehicles. The most distinctive feature of the stock was the flared skirt on the lower body-side which eliminated door footsteps and thus the possibility of late passengers trying to board a moving train. The interiors featured forced air ventilation. One of the major differences between O and P stock was that the guard's door operation position was provided in the driving cab on the former but on the latter was found at the inner end of one of the motor coaches.

The traction control apparatus featured a device known as a Metadyne machine which accelerated the motors of the train under the drivers control but without the need for traction resistances as had been the case on all previous stock. This development went on to prove troublesome in service and was removed in the mid-1950 when the trains were converted to standard camshaft and resistance control equipment that had proved successful on the 1938 stock. When converted the stock was re-classified as either CO or CP.

The units were first used on the Hammersmith & City and Uxbridge and Watford sections of the Metropolitan Line but during the course of their lives they also saw service on the District and Circle lines as well. The last sets ran in passenger service in March 1981.

CP Stock DM 53269 leaving Stamford Brook on 9 September 1975. *(Basil Hancock)*

A CO/CP Stock train at Earls Court on 9 September 1975. *(Basil Hancock)*

Q27 4379 trails an East London line service leaving New Cross on 3 November 1970. *(Basil Hancock)*

District Line Q Stock Programme

The Q stock programme started in 1938 and was devised to modernise the District Line fleet that comprised of many different types of vehicles of varying vintages. The idea being to eliminate the oldest stock on the line and bring all stock built from 1923 onward up to more modern standard. The Q stock programme involved very little new building of vehicles at all compared to the number of existing cars that were to be upgraded.

The reclassifying of units involved fitting them with air operated sling doors complete with passenger door control, electro pneumatic brakes with retardation control and making all stock fully compatible. In order to be able to dispose of all the pre-1920 built stock, twenty-five new driving motor and 183 new trailer cars were built and these featured identical body shells as used on the O and P stock. The new Q stock motor cars did not feature the Metadyne machine but more tried and tested relay and resistance type traction control.

Even after the programme was complete it was still possible to see Q stock trains running on the District Line with vehicles of no fewer than six different types in their formation. The last Q stock ran on the East London Line in 1971.

R38 22606 in painted silver livery compares with CP 54244 at Ealing Broadway on 10 September 1975. *(Basil Hancock)*

Painted R49 DM 22682 leads a train into Barking on 17 March 1979. *(Basil Hancock)*

Interiors of R49 DM 22681. *(Basil Hancock)*

R Stock

After the Second World War the District drew up plans to replace the large number of older units that still operated on the Circle Line and to replace District Line vehicles destroyed by enemy action during the war. The R stock used the same internal and external arrangement as the O and P stock but there the similarities ended. The new class was going to set new standards for EMU construction and design. To start with all vehicles in the units were motor coaches, one axle on each bogie being motorised. All R stock featured similar internal layout to O and P stock but with fluorescent lighting. The trains were built as six- and two-car sets, the former had a driving cab on each outer end but the two-cars only had the cab at one end as they were required to be detached during off peak periods when passenger loadings were lower. All but six of the driving motor cars of the first batch of R stock which was delivered in 1949 (but referred to as R47 stock) were converted from 1938 built Q stock motor coaches.

The second batch of R stock cars delivered in 1952 (known as R49 stock) featured a new development in EMU construction in the use of aluminium alloy for the body and frame work of the vehicles. Some non-driving and driving motor coaches of this second batch were converted from 1938 Q stock cars. During the delivery of this batch an experiment was carried out in leaving one newly built car unpainted so that it ran in a bare aluminium finish rather than LT train red. It was found that few difficulties arose with this and it was decided to form a complete eight-car formation of unpainted cars. In due course this became the preferred livery for all new LT trains from the 1950s onward; the classic underground silver train look was thus created which would last for four decades. A third and final batch of R stock was built in 1959 (R59 stock). As the converted Q stock cars were originally built of steel it was necessary to paint them in an aluminium finish to match the unpainted exterior of the new build R stock cars.

During 1971 the R stock were reformed into seven-coach trains and the detaching of the two-car sets during off-peak periods ceased. The last R stock ran in service in 1983.

Interior of Metro-Cammell 1956 prototype Tube Stock motor car 1000 on 6 April 1987. These cars could be distinguished from the 1959/1962 production cars by the wooden strip across the waist rail of the draught screen. In these cars these were painted metal. *(Basil Hancock)*

Interior of 1967 Tube Stock motor car 3177 on 26 March, 1987. *(Basil Hancock)*

1956/59/62 Tube Stock

In order to cope with a build up of traffic on the Central and Piccadilly lines new stock was required to replace the last of the 'Standard' stock still in use on these lines in the 1950s. In order to evaluate different ideas for the new builds three seven-car trains were ordered, one from each of the main builders of the time; Met-Cam, BRC&W and Gloucester RC&W. The trains were made up of a three- and a four-car unit as per the 1938 stock. All of the trains were roughly identical with differences only in their electrical equipment. The internal layout was exactly that of the 1938 stock and the external layout differed from that stock only in respect of a more flat front and the use of aluminium alloy for the body skin, which was left unpainted as per the R49 stock. The main internal difference from the 1938 stock was the use of fluorescent strip lighting. The first use of rubber suspension was made on these trains which was incorporated into all subsequent designs. It was fair to say that the 1956 stock experimental trains were simply an advancement of the 1938 stock design.

The first production units built as a result of the 1956 stock trials began delivery in 1959 for use on the Piccadilly Line, these units were to all intents and purposes clones of the 1956 stock trains and were built by Met-Cam in three- and four-car units. The 1959 stock was transferred to the Northern Line from 1975 and continued in use on that line until the last examples were withdrawn from use in January 2000.

The 1962 stock was built in four-car units only by Met-Cam with BR Derby works building all the trailer cars. There were only slight detail differences between the 1959 and 1962 stock and the two were fully compatible. The first units arrived on the Central Line in early 1962 and their delivery enabled 'on loan' units of 1959 stock to be returned to the Piccadilly Line. The 1962 stock continued to work the Central Line until 1993 when they were displaced by new stock. Some were reallocated to the Northern Line where they lasted until November 1999.

1956 Stock car 1000 on the right contrasts with 1959 Tube Stock 1268 at High Barnet, 6 May 1987. *(Basil Hancock)*

1967 Stock 3077 at Hainault on the Woodford shuttle service on 6 August 1976. *(Basil Hancock)*

1967 Stock at Walthamstow Central, 26 March 1987. *(Basil Hancock)*

1959 and 1972 Stock at Morden Depot between duties.

A60/62 Stock

The Metropolitan line was electrified from Rickmansworth to Amersham, including the branch from Chalfont & Latimer to Chesham, from the 12 September 1960. The section of line north of Amersham was transferred to the control of British Railways and the Metropolitan trains ceased to serve stations north of Amersham. New stock was built to replace the remaining loco-hauled and EMU stock of F, T and CO/CP types. Designated A stock and built in two batches by Cravens of Sheffield. The units were made up of four-car sets formed of a pair of driving motor cars with two intermediate trailers between. The stock had the now standard unpainted aluminium alloy bodies and ran in eight car formations on the Metropolitan and four cars on the East London Line and the Chalfont to Chesham shuttle. In keeping with the Metropolitan's status as a long-distance service provider the seating was high backed in a transverse layout only and luggage racks were provided at cantrail height.

The first batch were classified as A60 stock and entered service on the Amersham line. The second batch were known as the A62 stock and were introduced from 1961 for the Uxbridge line. The two batches were nearly identical.

The whole fleet went through a heavy refurbishment during the 1990s with the body ends having windows set into them as a way of improving personal security on the underground and this went onto to become a feature of all future builds and refurbishment plans for existing stock. Some of the units were used to test proposed paint schemes for a new corporate livery for the underground along with examples of other surface and tube stock. Three liveries were trialled and they all involved the body being painted white with one variation having just the doors blue, another variation had the lower half of the body blue and doors being blue and the third variant had the doors red with a blue band along the lower portion of the body. In all variants the front of the cab was painted red. It was the third livery that was eventually adopted and applied to every underground train.

The A60/62 stock gave sterling service on the Metropolitan and the last example ran in September 2012, having given fifty-one years of service these were one of the longest serving electric units ever to have run in Britain.

An A Stock train at Watford in 1994.

Chapter 14

The Age of Silver

London is ideally suited for the construction of tube railways, more so than any other city due to its central area sitting above a strata of soft clay, known as London Clay. This makes the boring of new tunnels far less arduous. Had London sat on top of hard rock then it is likely the tube network would be far more streamlined due to the resultant increase in construction costs. The nature of the operation, whereby every line serves the city and busy suburbs has made it invaluable to the needs of London from the outset and thus the network was never subject to any Beeching style pruning during the 1950s or 60s like the main line railways above ground. Indeed while the Beeching report saw branch lines around Britain ripped up plans were advanced for the construction of new tube lines under London.

The construction of the Victoria tube line from Walthamstow Central to Brixton

C Stock at Wimbledon 1994.

1973 Stock at speed on the non-stop section of the Piccadilly.

A 1973 Stock unit at Aldwych.

was authorised in the early 1960s. It was opened in stages with the section from Walthamstow to Highbury & Islington being first on 1 September 1968 with the section from Highbury & Islington to Warren Street following exactly three months later. On 7 March 1968 the line opened from Warren Street to Victoria but the final section from Victoria to Brixton did not open for over two more years, finally being ready for business on 23 July 1971. The Victoria line stock (1967 stock) was a fresh design for the Underground and featured a more flush-bodied aluminium alloy car with better lighting and ventilation. Its most startling feature was automatic train operation (ATO) which had been trialled on sections of the District and Central lines. With this equipment the driver virtually 'supervises' the trains operation as acceleration and braking is undertaken by computer control. The driver still has the facility to override the ATO equipment if it is deemed necessary. Units of similar style designated 1972 stock were built for use on the Bakerloo and Northern line but do not have ATO.

The Circle Line is one of the underground's busiest lines in terms of passenger numbers and it was decided to equip it with new trains in the late 1960s and increase train formations from five to six coaches. The new stock built for the line, designated C69 stock followed the now standard practice of having unpainted aluminium bodies but the new departure was to have four pairs of sliding doors on each side of the vehicles to enable faster loading and unloading at the stations. The new stock was to be shared with the Hammersmith & City line and maintained at the depot at Hammersmith. 106 two-coach units were built, each of which comprised a driving motor coach and a trailer. The motor coaches had four motors, one on each axle and three units would be coupled together in a M-T-T-M-T-M formation to work both lines. These units feature less seating than previous types in an effort to increase standing space, it being recognised that most journeys on the Circle are only a few minutes in duration. What seating there is was arranged in a mix of longitudinal and transverse style. A second batch of this stock, designated C77, was built in 1977 to replace older stock on the District line's Wimbledon to Edgware Road service.

The whole fleet was refurbished in the 1990s with all the seating changed to longitudinal type, reducing the number of seats further, along with the provision of windows in the carriage ends and the change from all silver to the new London Underground corporate livery.

The Piccadilly had taken over the running of the old District branch from Hammersmith to Hounslow West in 1933 and this line once more became a focus of attention when it was proposed to extend it to Heathrow Airport. The first section of this opened from Hounslow West station (which was fully rebuilt at a slightly different location) to Hatton Cross on 19 July 1975. The line was further extended with a loop line serving a station for Heathrow Airport Terminals 1, 2 & 3 on 16 December 1977. A station was added on the loop to serve the Terminal 4 building in 1984.

Connected with this extension the Piccadilly received brand new units of 1973 stock of similar style to the 1967 and 1972 stock units but without ATO and with a new type of electric braking system. To keep up with the expansion of Heathrow airport itself a new spur serving Terminal 5 had to be constructed off of the loop serving Terminals 1, 2, 3 and 4 and this opened on 27 March 2008.

D78 Stock and train at Wimbledon in 1994.

The District line was authorised to be re-equipped with new stock to replace the CO/CP and R stock in the late 1970s. It was classified as D78 stock and comprised of seventy-five six-car trains built by Metro-Cammell at their Washwood Heath plan, where so many previous stock for the underground lines had been constructed. The vehicles were the longest built for any underground line at sixty feet. This was to take advantage of the District's lack of severe curved platforms and reduced the total cost of the new fleet as a six-car train of the new stock was almost as long as a seven-car train of the old, thus fewer vehicles needed to be built. Fifty-five of the trains were formed of two three-car sets with a driving cab at one end and coupled back to back. Each three-car portion was formed of a driving motor, a trailer and a non-driving motor. Additionally a further twenty three-car units were built that had the non-driving motor replaced with another driving motor, making these double ended units capable of either operating individually or being coupled to the non-driving end of a single cabbed unit to make up a six-car.

The chassis and body work was made of aluminium with fluorescent lighting and a mixture of longitudinal seating at vehicle ends with an isolated section of face-to-face transverse seating in the centre of each car. The vehicles have four passenger doors on each side, one departure from previous builds was to make the doors single leaf. This makes the doorway slightly narrower than double leaf doors but the door itself is larger and requires larger operating air pistons mounted under the seats either side. Melamine panelling was used throughout and fire retardant foam was used in the seats. One feature that did carry over from previous stock was the slatted wooden flooring. The units were fitted with two motor alternator sets to provide the various voltages needed for train systems. The one

A train of 1983 Tube Stock on a Jubilee Line service heading north through Wembley.

1960 Stock at Ongar in the last weeks of service.

fitted under the trailer car feeds the 250 volt supply used on for the ventilation whilst the one on the driving motor coach supplies 48 volts D.C. For battery charging, control circuits and 115 volts A.C. For train lighting. Each motor coach is fitted with four traction motors and each driving motor coach additionally having the compressor fitted below the solebar, meaning the double ended units have two of these devices.

The first units entered service in January 1980 and the final units were delivered in 1983. The fleet has spent all of its time of the District line with the double ended units having a brief stint on the East London Line in the late 1980s. A plan for refurbishing the units was drawn up in 2001 and a prototype set was completed. It would take just over four years for the programme of works to refurbish the entire fleet to get under way and this was not completed until March 2008. These were the last trains in service in the unpainted aluminium livery as during refurbishment the vehicles were painted in the new corporate London Underground livery. Other work undertaken during the programme included the provision of new floors, replacement of the melamine with a new green and white Formica, provision of vehicle end windows, dot matrix destination displays, CCTV and replacement of some of the seats with tip up seating to provide space for universal access. At the time of writing all of the trains remain in service but their replacement is planned for 2015.

Jubilee Line

The construction of a new tube line in Central London from Baker Street to Charing Cross was proposed as early as 1965 under the Fleet Line name. Construction work on this project was authorised to start in 1971 and involved to boring of a new tunnel with intermediate stations at Bond Street and Green Park and ending at a newly built terminus on the north side of the Strand at Charing Cross station. This was never intended to be the final end of the line and the initial concept was that eventually the line would be extended east to Fenchurch Street and from there link up to the East London Line. North from Baker Street the line would take over the existing Bakerloo service from Baker Street to Stanmore. The name of the line was changed to Jubilee Line in 1977 to coincide with the silver jubilee of Queen Elizabeth II which was celebrated in that year. The line opened from Stanmore to Charing Cross on 30 April 1979. The ceremony was performed by Charles, Prince of Wales. Echoing the opening of London's first tubes that his ancestor, Edward VII had carried out when he was Prince of Wales.

When initially opened the 1972 tube stock was used to provide the service but this was only a temporary measure until a new fleet of fifteen six-car trains were provided, these were the 1983 stock. The original plan was for thirty units but a reduction in traffic saw the order placed with Metro-Cammell halved. An upsurge in patronage to the line meant that the additional fifteen trains were eventually required and were ordered as batch two in 1985. The design of the unit was best described as a tube-sized version of the D78 stock built for the District line as they shared many features such as the Aluminium frame and bodywork, the large single leaf passenger doors, the melamine interior and traction equipment. The formation was the same too being Driving Motor – Trailer – Non Driving Trailer – Non Driving Trailer – Trailer – Driving Motor. The 1983 stock did not achieve the level of reliability that its surface cousin did and the single leaf doors did not lend themselves to tube operations as well as they did on the surface lines. The stock was proposed for refurbishment in the late 1990s when an extension to the Jubilee line was authorised. It transpired that it would work out cheaper to build new trains than to re-engineer the 1983 stock to the standard needed and the whole fleet was withdrawn from traffic by July 1998.

While the London Underground had never experienced the widespread closures that removed thousands of stations from the British Railways map it was not to approach the new millennium without some changes, Back in the 1970s the Great Northern & City line, by now the Highbury branch of the Northern Line was transferred to British Rail, reversing the trend of Underground railways taking over main line company routes. The line was rebuilt by BR with third rail electrification and today forms the southern end of the Northern City line operated under the First Capital Connect franchise with services going to Welwyn Garden City and Hertford North.

In the 1960s the patronage of the Epping–Ongar line at the very eastern end of the Central line was still very low. The limitations on housing development in the area due to green belt restrictions and the rise in car ownership had put paid to any widespread surge in demand for direct train services to central London. The line suffered numerous cutbacks to the service, including the closure of Blake Hall station in 1981 and as the 1990s started it was clear the line was never going to pay its way. It was closed on 30 September 1994 and is now in private hands and run as a successful heritage railway.

The other branch that closed was the short one on the Piccadilly line from Holborn to Aldwych. It had been opened in 1907 when the station was called Strand and operated almost entirely as a shuttle from Holborn, with the exception of a very few through trains provided in the evenings for theatregoers up until 1908. The station was only served during peak hours from 1962 and the cost of refurbishing the station in the early 1990s made it uneconomic to remain open given its low patronage. The branch officially closed on 30 September 30 1994. The station building is Grade 2 listed and has been mothballed. It remains connected to the network and sees a lot of use as a location for filming, both for television and cinema. It could be argued that it has generated more revenue from this use than it ever did from ticket sales.

As the 1990s progressed the subject of improving public transport, both in the capital and beyond became something of a political football. Votes could be won from presenting a progressive transport policy and who should implement that policy would change the make-up of London's Underground in the biggest shake up since the formation of the London Passenger Transport Board some sixty years earlier.

Chapter 15

Transport for London

Following the abolition of the Greater London Council in 1984, London Regional Transport (LRT) was formed with responsibility for all public transport in Greater London. It was this organisation that oversaw the privatisation of bus routes and the introduction the Capitalcard scheme that allowed zonal travel on Tube, bus and British Railway's trains. LRT was also responsible for the construction of the Docklands Light Railway. Its operation of the entire underground was vested in a subsidiary called London Underground Limited from 1985.

The Jubilee Line extension was prompted by the re-development of the London Docklands and the Isle of Dogs that had already prompted the construction of the Docklands Light Railway which opened in 1987. This largely open air line linked the new commercial districts together and provided access to Central London connections at Bank and Tower Hill. Due to the nature of the DLR's operation there was no possibility with through running and what was needed was a direct connection with the new developments and the City. After a period of surveys and reports a scheme was put forward to extend the Jubilee from Green Park to Stratford via Greenwich and Canary Wharf. The plans gained parliamentary approval in 1992 and again with amendments in 1993 with work commencing in December 1993. The method of tunnelling was a new system developed in Austria and known as the Sequential Excavation Method (SEM). In this method the rock is cut away and underpinned by bolts, mesh and steel ribbing as the type of strata demands before a final lining of pre-cast concrete segments is installed. A concern over this method was brought about when a section of tunnel being dug the same way on the Heathrow–Paddington link collapsed in October 1994 and Jubilee work was suspended while the cause was investigated.

All of this was adding not only delays to the project but also pushing up the cost. There was another factor in getting the line on time that emerged when the site on the Greenwich Penninsular was chosen as the location for the Millennium Dome and would be the focal point for London's official celebrations for the start of the new millennium in 2000. In the end the line was opened in phases during spring and autumn 1999, working back from Stratford to North Greenwich in May, North Greenwich to Waterloo in September, with intermediate stations at London Bridge opened in October and Southwark in November. The final section to link up to a junction with the original Jubilee north of Charing Cross opened on 22 December 1999, just in time for all important new millennium party. This left the terminus at Charing Cross redundant

The Waterloo & City line was transferred over to London Underground in 1994. Just over a year earlier the stock built by the Southern Railway, to replace the original units on this line, had been retired. *(British Railways)*

Experimentally liveried A60 Stock at work on the East London Line in 1994.

and the Jubilee station was closed to passengers, but like Aldwych was retained in mothballed state and has been used for filming work.

The Jubilee line extension had been achieved but was not only late, it was hugely over budget. It did give London a glimpse of what the underground of the future will look like. The most noticeable change on the platforms was the provision of a glass barrier to prevent people either jumping or falling on the track. The barrier has doors that line up with the doors on the train and open in synchronisation with them. The stations were designed to be very spacious, unlike the original underground stations and the line has won architectural awards. A new depot was provided at Stratford and a new fleet of trains which featured ATO, like that used on the Victoria line.

The Jubilee Line extension was conceived and constructed against a backdrop that was a political battlefield. The Conservative government of the 1990s under John Major were pushing for more private involvement in transport and had privatised British Rail. One effect of that was the transfer of the Waterloo & City line from British Rail to LRT ownership in 1994. The Underground was not considered for the same treatment as British Rail but private investment was seen by the government as essential for future development of the network. The creation of a Public Private Partnership (PPP) was the government's way of achieving it. Under the PPP the assets of the Jubilee, Northern and Piccadilly Lines were transferred to Tube Lines Holdings. The Central, Victoria and Bakerloo Lines, as one group and the surface lines as another were transferred to Metronet Rail. These privately owned companies were responsible for the maintenance, upgrade and renewal of the routes in their group. The train service continued to be provided by London Underground but both public and private money was invested into the PPP groups. While all of this was being arranged there was not only a change in Government with the election of Tony Blair's New Labour in 1997. In 2000 a new local government was introduced in Greater London with the introduction of the introduction of the London Assembly. At the same time a new position of Mayor of London was created to effectively chair the Assembly. This created a huge political quagmire as both the Labour government and the new Mayor, Ken Livingstone, had been opposed to the idea of a PPP when in opposition. Once elected the establishment of it was too far advanced to stop and it came into being in 2002. By way of extra complication the role of London Regional Transport had passed to a new organisation directly responsible to the London Assembly and the Mayor, Transport for London (TfL).

By 2003 TfL had responsibility for running London Underground Services whilst the PPP groups owned and maintained the infrastructure and trains. TfL also managed the provision of the DLR, bus route regulation, implementation of the concession charge, tram services, major road routes, river services and the London Transport Museum in Covent Garden to name but a few. The alliance between TfL and the PPP was an uneasy one and many commentators expected the relationship was never going to last long. Metronet was the first of the PPP groups to fall down, it went into receivership in July 2007. In May 2008 all of its assets and responsibilities were passed back into public control by being vested with TfL. Tube Lines fared a little better but it was suffering a funding shortfall and its assets were bought out by TfL in May 2010. The

PPP came to an expensive end, the true cost, estimated in billions, to the UK taxpayer is still subject to an investigation by The National Audit Office.

Transport for London, now under a new mayor, Boris Johnson from May 2008, has invested heavily in a programme of upgrading the Underground network. This is to ensure they meet all the obligations they inherited from the PPP era. Some changes have been made to the network's running, the one that needs to be mentioned in this volume is the creation of the London Overground network of railway lines. It was made up of mainly routes in Greater London that have passed from ATOC operation to London Overground and include the ex-L&NWR lines from Euston to Watford, Richmond to Stratford and the Barking Gospel Oak line, the last is unusual as it is operated by diesel traction and is thus the only non-electric rail service under the control of TfL. Other lines that have joined the London Overground are the Clapham Junction to Willesden Junction route, part of which had been operated by the Metropolitan and the District back in the days of steam. The largest changes that brought about the completion of the London Overground involved the East London Line, including Marc Brunel's original Thames Tunnel. The whole route was closed for nearly two and a half years whilst it was rebuilt, including conversion from fourth rail to third rail electrification. It is now integrated into an enlarged route that runs from either Clapham Junction, West Croydon or Crystal Palace and links into the old East London Line at New Cross Gate (New Cross still remains another southern terminus), then follows the original formation to Shoreditch where a new route is taken to link up with the North London Line at Dalston. This has created a network that encircles London but services are operated in sections and not in a continuous loop like the circle line.

During this period it was decided that the entire fleet of trains on the surface lines and most of the tube lines would need replacement. This allowed the underground to acquire the most modern trains the market could offer, changing the outline of London's underground trains for the twenty-first century.

Chapter 16

The Trains of the Future

In a move that echoed the introduction of the 1938 tube stock, the replacement of the 'silver train' age stock began with the evaluation of three similar prototype trains. All were constructed as four-coach units made up of two identical back-to-back pairs comprised of a driving motor and a non-driving motors marshalled between them. Only two train builders participated in the trial; Met-Cam built two sets and BREL built the third. They were identified by a simple system of colour being applied to their doors, cab fronts and lower body-side, The rest of the body was painted white. The Met-Cam sets were green and red respectively while the BREL unit was light blue.

The design brief called for lightweight construction which dictated the use of aluminium. The lighting was fluorescent and the interior had to be 'roomy'. In a move not seen since the stock used on the C&SLR all seating was provided longitudinally. The largest departure from previous builds was the provision of doors that opened along runners on the outside of the body, and learning from the experience of the Jubilee stock the doors were double leaf with extra wide openings. The interior design of these trains recognised that at peak times it was more important to get more standing passengers inside the train than to try, in vain, to offer more seats. Tube journeys were on the whole comparatively short and those travellers who boarded at the furthest points away would get seats leaving only those who joined the train later and nearer the destination standing. This was the acceptable face of commuting in the late twentieth century and would remain the blueprint from thereon in.

Traction equipment differed between the three trains, DC motors were still used by controls were by thyristors with micro-processors used extensively. On the Met-Cam trains one set was fitted with GEC made motors, the other with equipment supplied by Brown-Boveri of Zurich. The BREL train had its traction equipment supplied by Brush of Loughborough.

The trains ran on test from 1986 and also in passenger use on the Jubilee from 1988. All three were withdrawn by 1990 and placed in store, eventually being broken up except for a single car of the green train which was saved for the London Transport Museum.

The Central Line was the first line to benefit from the new breed of trains when it received the first deliveries of 1992 Tube Stock. These were based on the BREL prototype train and were made up of four two-car sets but with the ones in the middle of the formation having on shunting driving cab controls and not full size cabs. The

Above: A train of 2009 Tube Stock enters Oxford Circus, southbound. *Below:* 1995 Stock on a northbound Northern Line service at Charing Cross, January 2014.

A train of S Stock on an eastbound Hammersmith & City Line service at Paddington, December 2013. *(Graeme Gleaves)*

traction equipment was provided by a consortium of Brush and ABB and featured not only micro-processor control and thyristors but also control lines they worked on fibre optics, a first for a UK EMU fleet. Provision was made for ATO. Features introduced on this stock that were to become a standard for all future builds included automatic announcements and dot matrix destination displays, both on the front and inside the cars. Some of the seats around the doorways were the tip up type, this allowed either more standing room or a space for wheelchair users with universal access provision regulations being introduced in the near future this was some good forward thinking. Also there were 'perching' seats which are padded for standing passengers to lean against.   [space for 1 image to come]

The units were introduced from April 1993. Near identical units were purchased by British Rail for use on the Waterloo & City Line and these passed to London Underground along with the line in 1994.

The next two lines to be re-equipped were the Northern and the Jubilee. The former received the 1995 Tube Stock which was introduced into traffic from 1997, while the Jubilee stock was designated 1996 Tube stock and introduced from 1997 in readiness for the opening of the Jubilee line extension. Both stocks are essentially the same design with the main difference being the make of traction equipment fitted to them. The designs were the first trains on the Underground to make use of three phase AC traction motors. These are smaller than the previously used DC ones and are fed from an AC supply created by feeding the DC current from the conductor rail into an inverter that converts it to AC pulses needed for traction. These new propulsion systems have changed the 'sound of the Underground' as the traditional growl and low-pitched whine of the DC traction motor has been replaced on these lines with the high-pitch whine of a traction inverter and the equipment switching through the frequencies. Both types were built as six-car units with a formation of Driving Motor – Trailer – Non Driving Motor – Non Driving Motor – Trailer – Driving Motor; the non-driving motors are equipped with controls to facilitate uncoupling and shunting in depots at their inner bulkhead where they couple to each other. The Jubilee Line sets were extended to seven coaches in January 2006 with a newly built trailer car being put into each train formation.

The final Tube line to be equipped for now is the Victoria Line. This was done with the provision of forty-seven eight-car units of 2009 Tube Stock. The trains were built by Bombardier at Derby and the first sets entered service from July 2009. The trains are formed of a Driving Motor – Trailer, Non Driving Motor – Uncoupling Non Driving Motor – Uncoupling Non Driving Motor – Non Driving Motor – Trailer – Driving Motor. They also feature three-phase drive with AC traction motors, which is the standard for all new EMUs in Britain. Like all trains introduced after the prototype trains of 1986 the doors are on the outside of the body and comprise of two double leaf sets on the body sides a third of the way into each end with a single leaf door on each end with the exception of the driving motors. The 2009 stock differs in that the doors are slightly wider and the driving cab has its own external crew door. The introduction of this stock coincided with renewal of the Victoria Line's signalling system and ATO equipment. The 2009 fleet, like the 1967 fleet before it, continues to be maintained at the line's dedicated depot at the northern end of the line in Northumberland Park.

The last new stock to be covered in this volume is the S stock. This fleet is designed to replace all the existing designs on the surface lines and is a standard type, so the S either stands for 'surface' or 'standard'. The trains are formed into either eight-car formations for the Metropolitan (S8) or seven-cars for the Circle and Hammersmith & City (S7). The trains will enter service on the District Line in seven-car formation but at the time of writing this part of the programme has yet to start. The Metropolitan was fully changed over to S8 stock during 2012 and the C Stock on the Circle and Hammersmith and City Line will be completely replaced by S7 formations in 2014. The introduction of these trains will see an eventual rise in the traction current supplied from 630 to 750 volts DC.

The design of the trains is a surface version of the 2009 Tube Stock but with all vehicles motored and the seating does have a mix of transverse and longitudinal as well as tip up and perching seats. The two firsts that feature on these trains are air conditioning and the facility to walk through the entire train (legitimately) with open car end vestibule connections. The trains also feature regenerative braking whereby the train's motors are used in the retardation of the train and the energy they create during this is returned to the conductor rail to reduce energy consumption.

The London Underground is now the operator of some of the most state-of-the-art electric trains in Britain, but then it is fair to say that as an all-electric railway, whoever operated it, the Underground has always been at the front of the queue in engaging new technology. The replacement of the Bakerloo and Piccadilly lines in the next decade will see even more innovations.

Control room and generator hall of the Lots Road Power Station, which opened in 1905. *(JC)*

Chapter 17

Power to the System

In this final chapter I will examine the means by which the Underground's massive daily demand for electricity has been met. Back in 1890 there was no national grid to take a supply from and so the C&SLR, like all early railway electrification schemes, had to take the step of building their own power station to meet their energy requirements. The C&SLR built theirs at Stockwell and as previously described it was driven by steam produced in Lancashire Boilers, pressurised and then fed to drive stationary compound steam engines which in turn drove dynamos that produced the electricity that was fed directly to the conductor rail at 500 volts DC. The boilers were powered by coal and this had to be delivered to the railway then transferred below ground to the power station. This process was very hungry for both coal and water and it was a necessity of the design of any power station that the means to supply both of these were of primary concern. The arrangement was the same when the Waterloo & City and Central London Railways built their power stations.

The big change for the Central London Railway was the need to have sub-stations positioned along their route to keep the voltage supply to the conductor rail 'topped up'. The CLR's power station was at the western end of their line at Wood Lane, near Shepherd's Bush. One of the properties of electricity is that when supplied to a conductor, like the conductor rails used by the Underground it will flow, but all conductors have a level of in-built resistance; that is the amount they will inhibit the flow of electrons along its length. All metals conduct electricity but some are better at it than others, the better ones tend to be the most expensive precious metals so making conductor rails out of these would render railway electrification financially impractical. It was to get around this that sub-stations were installed along the route. These are essentially junction boxes fed by high conducting feeder cables from the power station which then in turn put the current, still at a the supply voltage into the conductor rail. The use of sub-stations has been universal in all railway electrification projects. Without them a train would simply run out of a usable voltage the further it travelled from the source of power. By breaking the line into sections, each with their own dedicated feed, this problem is negated.

When the large scale electrification of the District came into being under the auspices of the UERL group the need for a larger power station was obvious and a site was chosen at Lots Road in Chelsea on the north bank of the River Thames. Here there was a plentiful supply of water, not from the Thames but from an underground well, and

Bogie of R38 DM 22662 showing collectors shoe. The porcelain insulators that support the live rail are clearly visible.

Left: The conductor rail is fed from heavy-duty cables needed to withstand the large currents drawn by electric traction, these can be seen at this break in the live rails. Just visible on the wall are the additional cables that run through the tunnels carrying feeds for lighting, signalling, communications and traction.

the Chelsea Wharf would enable coal to be delivered by barge. The site had originally been identified by the Brompton & Piccadilly Circus Railway for their tube line. That concern came under the control of the UERL group in 1901 and along with it came their power station plans. Lots Road power station would go on to supply electricity to not only all of the UERL group but almost the whole of London Transport's electric transport network, which in the 1920s and 1930s included tram and trolley bus routes.

The power station's boilers were fitted with condensing apparatus that enabled most of the steam to be recycled after cooling to be boiled again. For this process the water from the river was used as a cooling agent, it was estimated that at its peak of operation some fourteen million pounds of water were boiled every day. The coal boilers were fed by mechanical stokers and a total of 750 tons of coal was burned daily, four chimneys were provided for the exhaust gasses. This changed in the 1960 when the station was converted from coal burning to oil burning and two of the chimneys were demolished as redundant. A little over a decade later and Lots Road was again converted to take advantage of the newly discovered North Sea gas, it retained the option of oil firing should the supply of gas be interrupted for any reason. At its peak the station was capable of producing just over 100,000 kilowatts; all of which were distributed and monitored under the watchful eye of the staff in the stations control room. In the 1990s Lots Road was becoming due for re-equipment, and pre-dating the national grid it was one of the oldest power stations still in operation. The national grid had, however,

Ealing Common depot on 10 September 1975. Visually similar Q38, CO/CP and R Stock trains are all in this view. *(Basil Hancock)*

A Watford Junction-bound 1972 Stock train leaving Headstone Lane on 21 July 1978. These units were only used on the Bakerloo for a brief period before delivery of the line's dedicated replacement fleet. *(Basil Hancock)*

caught up with the needs of transport, which meant it was now more cost effective for the Underground to take their power from there than to renew their own station. Lots Road was shut down on 21 October 2002. It was the last dedicated railway power station left operating in Britain and so this marked the end of an era that had started in Stockwell in 1890. At the time of writing the site is subject to a planning application that will see the old buildings demolished and a residential and retail construction is planned to take its place.

Before leaving the subject of power supply mention need to be made of the dual operation between trains of the Underground, which run on the four rail system and those of the former Southern Region of British Rail that work on the third rail system. With four rail a positive conductor rail is placed outside of the track gauge and collector shoes mounted on the bogies of the train make contact with this and feed the train's electrical equipment. Once this has been done the negative return needed to complete the circuit is sent back to another set of collector shoes mounted under the bogie which is in contact with a negative conductor rail that then takes the feedback to the sub-station and the circuit is complete. On the Underground the difference between the two conductor rails is 630v DC. On the Southern region the system is similar up to the point whereby the negative return is not fed to a dedicated conductor rail but is fed into the running rails which act as the return path. This system was employed on both the C&SLR and the CLR until they were converted to the Underground standard of four rail. The different nature of the operation would not be a problem as each of them has their own dedicated lines, but there were three locations where both third and fourth rails trains had to operate. These are the lines north of Queens Park on the Bakerloo and the District sections from Putney Bridge to Wimbledon and Gunnersbury to Richmond. The means by which the inter running is achieved is a very simple fix. The dual lines are set up as normal third rail lines and are fed by Network Rail's system of power supply. To enable the underground trains to operate the negative conductor rail is also provided but rather than connect it directly to the negative feed it is linked by bonds to the running rails and thus four rail trains will make the circuit they need.

The low voltage DC system has worked well for urban railways, whilst high voltage AC overhead line is now the system of choice for the main line railways due to its ability to support higher voltage, higher current and high speed running and noises are now being made about using the system to replace the third rail network south of London to the coast; the four rails of the underground will continue to be the power behind London for many, many years to come.

Above: Painted R49 DM 22682 leads a train into Barking on 17 March 1979. *Below:* 1938 Stock train with car 11263 leading at Finchley Central on 8 September 1975. *(Basil Hancock)*

Further Reading

This book aims to provide an overview of the story behind the creation of our electric Underground and the development of the electric trains that have run on it. If you would like to find out more about any aspect of the history or science behind these stories then fortunately there are a number of superb books which have been published over the years on various aspects of the system, its tunnels and its trains. Many of these were used in the reference work for this book and the author has no hesitation in recommending them.

General History:
Rails Through the Clay by Alan A. Jackson & Desmond F. Croome. Published by Taylor Francis Ltd in 1962, re-released in 1993 and again in 2013 in paperback. ISBN: 9780415860468
This is regarded by many aficionados as the definitive history of the Underground and is a weighty volume. Not for the casual observer, this one is certainly for the enthusiasts.

London's Underground by H. F. Howson. Published by Ian Allan Ltd in 1951, 1959, 1961 and 1967
One of the first books ever published by Ian Allan this volume has a good overview of the early years. Later editions bring the story up to date as developments were made and the last edition covers the construction and equipping of the Victoria Line in some detail.

London's Underground by John Glover.
Published by Ian Allan Ltd in and now in its eleventh edition. ISBN: 0-7110-1899-5
Covers the history from the steam years up to the present day and is wonderfully illustrated. A must have for any Underground fan.

Individual Lines:
The Twopenny Tube by J. Graeme Bruce and Desmond F. Croome. Published by Capital Transport in 1996. ISBN: 1854141864
The complete story of the Central London Railway and how it became the Central Line. Covers both infrastructure, rolling stock and the behind the scenes politics.

The City & South London Railway by T. S. Lascelles. Published by The Oakwood Press in 1955 and re-released in 1987. ISBN: 0853613605
The definitive work on the history of the C&SLR from its inception to the take-over by UERL and its rebuilding. The locomotives, stock, station and operations are all examined in detail.

The Metropolitan District Railway by Charles E. Lee. Published by The Oakwood Press in 1956 and re-released in 1988. ISBN: 0853613613
Covers the District and its construction and early years. The boardroom battles with the Metropolitan and the period through electrification and take over by UERL right up to the formation of the LPTB.

M. A. C. Horne authored a series of books, published by Douglas Rose, on various underground lines, each simply called 'A Short History' and I have referenced *The Central Line* (1987 ISBN: 187035401X), *The Bakerloo Line* (1990 ISBN: 1870354052) and *The Northern Line* (1987 ISBN: 1870354001). These are very interesting reads, with reproductions of maps and diagrams that greatly assist with the text.

Rolling Stock:
For the current or recent fleets you should look no further the most recent edition of *London Underground Rolling Stock* by Brian Hardy. Published by Capital Transport each volume gives a description of the different types of unit in service as well as the support fleet that works on maintenance duties behind the scenes. Includes all unit formations and numbers.

Steam to Silver by J. Graeme Bruce. Published by Capital Transport in 1970 and revised in 1983. ISBN: 0904711455
This is the definitive work on the subject of surface lines stock and locomotives from the very beginning of the Metropolitan and the District, through electrification and up to the introduction of the D78 stock. Many rare photos and technical information.

London Underground Tube Stock by J. Graeme Bruce. Published by Ian Allan Ltd in 1988 (originally published as Tube Trains Under London in 1971). ISBN: 0711017077
Covers the story of the development of the tube train from the locomotives and carriages of the C&SLR up to the introduction of the 1973 Stock on the Piccadilly Line. Plenty of details of what is under the floor as well as the passenger accommodation.

London Underground Surface Stock Planbook 1863-1959 by Ian Huntley. Published by Ian Allan Ltd in 1988. ISBN: 0711017212
Aimed at the modellers as it features scale drawings in 4mm to the foot scale of the steam and electric locomotives, carriages and EMUs used on the District and Metropolitan during the years in the title. Notes on numbering and livery details, along with prototype photographs are also included.

1938 Stock trains passing at Queens Park on 9 May 1985. 10291 in 1938 livery and a set in 'Bus' red. *(Basil Hancock)*

Acknowledgements

I would like to thank the many people who have supported me in the production of this work, either through their direct contributions or their moral support which has kept me going to see the completion of this work, without them this would never have seen the light of day!

Firstly my colleagues at Vintage Electric Trains; Rob Davidson, John Missenden, Nick Evans, Dave Stretton and Brian Thompson for their loyal support, also Mark Bowman, for it was he who put me in touch with Basil Hancock who has kindly provided many images that are published in these pages fora the first time. I would also like to thank Clive Morris, Anthony Coulls and Richard Gibbon along with the other members of the Railway Heritage Register Partnership. Then of course there is my family; Sarah and Ben, Katharine, Marina, Floyd, Lyn and Richard for putting up with me and my artistic moods! Finally thanks to John Christopher and all at Amberley Publishing for putting their faith in me and giving me the chance to produce this work.

GNB&PR publicity material to promote their new service.